Preface

We chose to publish this academic study as a short book because we want it to be accessible to both academics and those working with, or affected by, offending and addiction. We hope the book offers practitioners some insight into their clients' experiences and, perhaps, as a result, new ways of supporting them might emerge. More optimistically, we hope that it will assist policymakers as they design and develop more compassionate, kind and sustainable policies to support individuals like the men in this study.

We also hope the book will help those struggling with active addiction, or even those whose loved ones are struggling, to gain some insight into where their addiction may have originated and learn what's worked for people who have travelled this road, who have hit rock bottom (more than once) and who have come out the other end to find peace of mind.

Early Life: Trauma and Masculinity

- The men interviewed as part of this study all suffered trauma as children. These traumas were often (con)founded in and by economic deprivation and social exclusion;
- Many participants dropped out of school because they experienced bullying by their peers and neglect by those in authority. This bullying and neglect was often exacerbated by the poverty and abuse they experienced at home;

- As the men had few pro-social role models growing up they looked up to local *hard-men* who taught them how to behave and survive in their community;
- The men coveted a hegemonic masculinity, known locally as being a *hard-man*. The men spent much of their early life trying to cultivate, and then maintain, hard-men reputations. This involved being violent, always being ready to aggress or retaliate against perceived insults and being involved in a range of risk-taking behaviours, including heavy drinking and drug use;
- This localised hard-man subculture was an outcome of economic deprivation and social exclusion, coupled with the absence of pro-social role models and often a lack of legitimate meaningful employment;
- Such hard-man images prohibited behaviour seen as weak, and this served as a barrier to success in school and the development of healthy coping mechanisms, such as talking. With no healthy outlets, drink and drug use became the primary means of suppressing/masking feelings.

Drug and Alcohol Use

- Drug and alcohol served a number of purposes. Initially, drugs/alcohols were used to fit in and, as a marker of masculine identity and status, and later to self-soothe. All participants in this study eventually entered active addiction;
- As adults, active addiction led to further trauma. Many participants reported experiencing assault, hospitalisation and abandonment as adults. Many reported their mental and physical health deteriorated significantly while in active addiction. Most thought about or attempted suicide, many overdosed: one participant in this study sadly died during the term of the research process.

Recovery and Desistance

- Recovery from addiction came before desistance from crime;
- Desistance from crime was seen as a *side effect* of overcoming addiction;
- Recovery was often a slow process, and all of the men experienced a *rocky road*, with several *rock bottoms* being reached on the journey;

- Rock bottom often involved a physical process (injury, illness etc.) but more importantly a loss of identity and sense of self. The men described losing their ability to maintain hard-fought masculine identities as they became too weak to engage in violence and were unable to stay in control of their emotions, their bodies and their relationships;
- For some of the men in this study, prison served a positive purpose. Incarceration helped cultivate the hard-man image when they were young. When older, prison gave the men respite from the chaos of their lives and provided access to services which were often the first step on their recovery journey;
- Recovery can be achieved without having to spend time in prison and access to services should not be dependent on spending time in prison. Appropriate services must be more readily available early and often in the community.
- The men all found much-needed support in 12-Step type programmes. These self-help groups provided not only a space to talk about emotions, often for the first time, but also pro-social role models, who demonstrated alternative forms of more positive masculinity;
- The men often needed to distance themselves from existing friends and family, whilst in recovery, however, total isolation in an effort to overcome addiction was seldom helpful;
- Whilst in recovery, the men needed to avoid what they called gateway behaviours, commonly identified as dishonesty (e.g. selling drugs), *womanising* (e.g. dishonesty in relationships), violence and gambling. The men described how engaging in such behaviours was a slippery slope away from a tentative recovery.
- Full recovery involved moving away from an identity based on hegemonic masculinity and the associated behaviours. Success meant leaving the hard-man identity behind and creating a new sense of self.
- Achieving recovery and desistance took time. Finding job and engaging in education were often aims that were not realistic in the early stages of recovery. These came later once the men had a chance to work on themselves.
- All the men in this study spoke about living a good and decent life and giving back to society. Ultimately, all of the men spoke about their experience as a journey out of chaos and their outcome was finding peace of mind (Fig. 1).

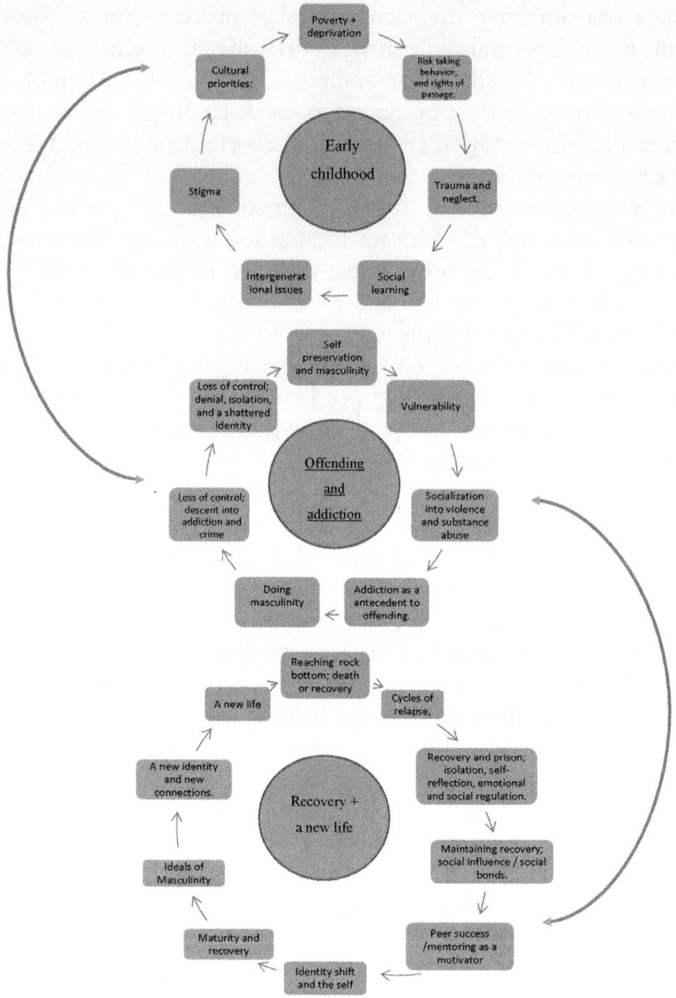

Fig. 1 The three-stage integrated cycles of recovery model

Cork, Ireland

Graham Cambridge
Orla Lynch
James Windle

Contents

1 Introduction 1

2 Desistance and Recovery in the Academic Literature 11

3 Cork City: Understanding the Context 23

4 Methodology 31

5 Traumatic Childhood and Adolescent Experiences 45

6 Lifestyle, Offending, and Addiction 63

7 Moving Out of the Chaos 97

8 Conclusion 135

References 153

Index 165

CHAPTER 1

Introduction

Abstract Over the past twenty years there has been an increase in research examining desistance, the process of passive and active desistance and interventions to support desistance. However, despite the well-established relationship between addiction and crime, there is a gap in the literature when it comes to a holistic understanding of the process of moving away from crime ***and*** addiction as interrelated processes. More recently there have been a number of studies that examine these processes from a cognitive and social perspective, but there is some distance to go conceptually and practically. This chapter lays the groundwork for a study that examines the processes of desistance and recovery from addiction amongst a sample of men who have spent time in Irish prisons. The chapter explores key concepts of relevance to the study, including addiction recovery and desistance and outlines the processes of data collection and analysis.

Keywords Addiction · Recovery · Desistance · Insider

Over the past twenty years there has been an increase in research examining desistance amongst specific populations, such as sex offenders (e.g. Cresswell, 2021) and perpetrators of political violence (e.g. Lynch, 2015). Despite the well-established relationship between addiction and crime,

G. Cambridge et al., *The Desistance Journey*,
https://doi.org/10.1007/978-3-031-11269-0_1

however, there is a gap in the literature when it comes to a holistic understanding of the population from whom the process of moving away from crime *and* recovery from addiction are interrelated processes (see Robinson & Hamilton, 2016; Roeyen et al., 2017). While many studies point to how recovery from addiction and desistance from drugs are overlapping processes, research into the area is relatively new (see Best & Colman, 2020).

This book began life as an examination into desistance from offending amongst men in County Cork—the largest county in the Republic of Ireland. With a population of over 500,000 people, the county is served by one male-only prison and, of the almost 300 men incarcerated in Cork prison, an estimated 70 per cent, are believed to have addiction issues (Pollak, 2017); anecdotal accounts put this number closer to 90 per cent. Given the profile of those incarcerated in Cork prison, and the fact that all of the men who agreed to participate in this study had addiction issues, the focus of the project quickly shifted to an investigation of the *bigger picture* of desistance: namely how offending and recovery from addiction were inseparable processes.

This book is based on in-depth interviews with 40 men from Cork who had engaged with the criminal justice system, most had served time in prison. The book traces the participants' life histories: from the hardships they endured as children, through the chaotic teenage years leading into active addiction, further hardship in adulthood, and the often numerous attempts at recovery and eventually, for most, full recovery. The interviews were conducted by the first author (Graham Cambridge), who was born and raised in the Northside of Cork City, an area of the city which has suffered the highest concentration of economic deprivation, crime and problematic drug use.

Graham undertook these interviews as an insider. As a child he experienced the economic deprivation felt by so many of the participants, he knew the streets the men spoke about and as a young adult, he understood the dynamics of the community. Graham brought this personal experience to bear on the research process and was able to communicate in a meaningful way with potential participants. His insider status was central to the data collection and analytical process and gave participants the sense that Graham understood where the men were coming from and, the interviewer and interviewee knew that they shared common connections from a time gone by. This may have been one reason why the participants opened up, and why so many shared traumatic life experiences during the interviews and trusted Graham with personal information. Being interviewed by a *local*, who had left school at 13 but was now studying for a Ph.D., and being interviewed inside the imposing nineteenth-century barricades of University College Cork helped participants widen their understanding of what was possible for 'people like us'. It showed to the men that further education was not just for the elite, but, that people from the Northside of Cork city could not only go to university but reach the peak of educational attainment. That is, the research upon which this book is based was designed to produce more than a book: it was designed to support those living with addiction and their communities by giving them hope for their future.

Graham is currently employed as an outreach worker supporting people in Cork city with addiction issues. As such, this book is intended to provide readers with a practice-friendly account of the academic work on desistance and a multidisciplinary holistic account of the process of *doing desistance and recovery*. While this book is academic in design, the voices of the participants are prioritised both to tell their stories in their own words but also to ground the recommendations discovered by the authors in real-world experiences. We hope that the book will help some people who are struggling with their addiction to understand how they got to where they are, understand how are currently feeling, understand that they are not alone and, most importantly, know that peace of mind is achievable. All but one of the 40 men in this study did eventually achieve the peace of mind they sought.

Addiction

The words used to describe particular drug-using behaviours are socially constructed, they are of a particular time and place and are sometimes unique to particular regions of the world; the terminology used is in a constant state of flux. Words that are deemed acceptable today are rejected tomorrow. A number of academics and practitioners are critical of historically used terms, particularly deficits based terms where the focus is on the individual e.g. addict. These terms are seen by some as stigmatising and dehumanising terms which strip the person of all other aspects of their identity. The men in this study are all more than their addiction, they were also sons and fathers, friends, builders and so much more. As such, many organisations and academics prefer first-person language which reminds us to focus on the whole person, for example, ***person with a substance use disorder*** (see Changing the Narrative, no date).

This said, the participants in this study referred to themselves as addicts and to avoid the words participants used to describe themselves would be dismissive of their experiences (see Leonard & Windle, 2020; Lynch et al., 2021). We acknowledge that the individuals themselves may be reflecting the negative language used about them when they use deficits-based language, but after consultation with the participants, we have chosen to mirror the language universally used by the men who participated in this study. We choose to respect their words and their choices.

The debate about terminology used for what has been routinely referred to as addiction is ongoing. The World Health Organisation (2018: no page) defines 'dependence syndrome' as:

> a cluster of behavioural, cognitive, and physiological phenomena that develop after repeated substance use and that typically include a strong desire to take the drug, difficulties in controlling its use, persisting in its use despite harmful consequences, a higher priority given to drug use than to other activities and obligations, increased tolerance, and sometimes a physical withdrawal.

Kleiman and colleagues (2011: 5) summarise this as a:

> … bad, unwanted, and hard-to-break habit, leading to a pattern in which someone repeatedly takes a drug more often, or in greater amounts, than she or he intends to.

Few people who use drugs go on to develop substance abuse disorders and even fewer become addicted, which Kleiman and colleagues (2011: 6) define as a 'chronic, relapsing disorder' in which the individual 'suffers … an enormous amount of damage'. This definition certainly fits the description of addiction provided by the men in this study.

Many other organisations now also focus on the ***harm*** (rather than the use itself), so use the term ***problematic drug use*** rather than addiction. This is defined by the European Monitoring Centre for Drugs and Drug Addiction (2020: no page) as:

> Recurrent drug use that is causing actual harms (negative consequences) to the person (including dependence, but also other health, psychological

or social problems), or is placing the person at a high probability/risk of suffering such harms.

Throughout this book we will refer to individuals who use drugs and alcohol problematically in this way, but where our participants have used the term addiction, we will reflect this in the relevant sections.

Recovery

Recovery is used in the colloquial sense to refer to a journey towards well-being, usually with the aid of some form of intervention. This does not cover the full meaning of what is entailed in recovery from problematic drug use or addiction. The Betty Ford Institute Consensus Panel (2007: 222) defined recovery as 'a voluntarily maintained lifestyle characterised by sobriety, personal health and citizenship'. This definition reflects the all-encompassing lifelong and sustained nature of recovery. Nonetheless, very few people problematically using drugs, or even those addicted to drugs, enter treatment: most stop naturally and some simply curtail their use without sobriety. Those entering treatment tend to be the minority where the harm to all aspects of their lives is comprehensive and uncontrollable. This book is about, and for, that relatively small number of people.

The Betty Ford Institute Consensus Panel (2007: 223) further differentiated the stages of recovery into "early sobriety" (the first year), "sustained sobriety" (between 1 and 5 years), and 'stable sobriety' (of more than 5 years). This alludes to a finding of this research: that the longer people are in recovery the more stable they are in their recovery. Addiction is progressive, the longer people are in active addiction the greater the mental, physical and emotional harm that occurs. Recovery is also progressive and the more time that individuals are in recovery, the longer they have to recover from the mental, physical and emotional harm experienced before they started their recovery.

Desistence

Desisting from crime is the process whereby someone with a history of criminal behaviour stops offending or reduces the severity or incidence of their offending behaviours; in other words they either stop offending or they engage in less serious crime less often. Like recovery, desistance is not a smooth path, and there are often periods of non-offending, followed by periods of offending and this pattern may continue for some time (Maruna, 2001; McNeill et al., 2012; Weaver & McNeill, 2007). The majority of desistance research has centred upon developmental and life-course criminology where the focus is most often on the developing adolescent, or the period of early adulthood; there is less focus on older adulthood (Sampson & Laub, 1993). Regardless of the developmental period studied, it is broadly recognised that desistance is a dynamic process of change where the ultimate outcome is that an individual stops committing crime.

At a very basic level for both men and women, there are three theoretical phases of desistance. The first, primary desistance, is the process of *stopping offending*, the physical act itself, often involving periods of non-offending. The second, secondary desistance, refers to the process of personal change where an individual commits to being a non-offender, in other words *not offending* becomes an important part of their identity (Maruna & Farrall, 2004). The third, tertiary desistance, refers to the recognition (or lack of) that a person has changed, and can be re/accepted into a group or community. The concept of tertiary desistance identifies that individual desistance requires community support (McNeill, 2016).

Chapter Outlines

This book largely follows the normal style of an academic book. Chapter 2 briefly assess the existing academic literature on desistance from crime, and the dual processes of desistance and rehabilitation from addiction. This chapter sets some theoretical foundations.

Chapter 3 provides the socio-economic context of the research site (Cork City). The chapter illuminates the transgenerational concentration of economic deprivation and social exclusion within a small number of areas. It discusses how a gradual process of deindustrialisation from the 1980s increased relative and absolute deprivation, and how inequalities increased during both economic boom (the Celtic Tiger) and bust (the Great Recession). The chapter concludes by reviewing the Irish criminological literature to suggest that the Irish prison population is over-represented by people coming from socially excluded and economically deprived areas.

Chapter 4 briefly introduces the methods used in this study. In summary, the first author conducted in-depth life history interviews with 40 men from Cork City who were involved with the criminal justice system. As the first author is an insider—he grew up in Cork's Northside and is now an outreach worker—the chapter concludes by discussing the importance and limitations of insider-research.

Chapter 5 explores the early years of the men's life histories, as presented by the participants. This chapter provides insight into how participants reconstruct their experience of early childhood and, how they experience and attribute motive to their early behaviours in light of their later engagement in crime and substance use. The men rationalise their adult behaviours by linking them to childhood experiences, notably: the shame and stigma they experienced in relation to their household poverty, the neglect they experienced as children and, violence and substance use they experienced or witnessed in the home. A central theme to emerge is that the shame and stigma of poverty spurred them to withdraw from school and mainstream community engagement, prompting a cascade of negative life events.

Chapter 6 addresses the broad area of lifestyle, offending and addiction. It begins by exploring the mens' teenage years, focusing specifically on thrill-seeking behaviour, but also how the lack of local pro-social role models resulted in the men looking up to local 'hard-men'. The men speak about what life was like growing up in their community and how it was dominated by violence, crime and addiction. They identified how their behaviours were responses to their environment and served strategic purposes. The men discussed cultivating hard-man identities as survival mechanisms to avoid being victimised and how they used alcohol and/or drugs to soothe the pain of the childhood traumas discussed in chapter three. The men also discuss how their behaviours were learnt through interacting with peer groups and family members, and imitation of local 'hard-men'. The men were eager to look at their behaviours and link them to their traumas of early childhood. This chapter documents how drink/drug use initially served a purpose—it helped the men to deal with the trauma, hurt, boredom and helplessness in their lives—but quickly became problematic as addiction overtook choice. The chapter concludes by discussing how the mens' lifestyle harmed their physical and mental health and often culminated in suicide attempts, overdoses and incarceration.

Chapter 7 follows the men's narratives as they journey to multiple rock bottoms, and outlines how they entered recovery in order to stay alive. This journey from active addiction to recovery is not straightforward. The journey, as retold by the men, was very difficult. They often experienced many relapses along the way. Each relapse brought them to a new low, which left them spiritually and mentally broken. Each of the men, however, showed great resilience and the lows provided the motivation to attempt recovery again. They also learned during this process where to find support. The chapter explores how the men, while in recovery and most notably in 12-Step Programmes, found role models that had been absent in their earlier lives. These role models taught the men not only to live a life without drink/drugs, but also how to live another form of masculinity, one which did not need performative displays of violence and aggression. The chapter also discusses some of the strategies the men adopted, and what they found useful to eventually find 'a bit of peace and happiness'.

References

Best, D., & Colman, C. (2020). *Strengths-based approaches to crime and substance use: From drugs and crime to desistance and recovery*. Routledge.

Betty Ford Institute Consensus Panel. (2007). What is recovery? A working definition from the Betty Ford Institute. *Journal of Substance Abuse Treatment, 33*(3), 221–228.

Cresswell, C. (2021). Giving voice to convicted perpetrators of sexual harm: Assisted desistance in the community. In O. Lynch, J. Windle, & Y. Ahmed (Eds.), *Giving voice to diversity in criminological research: Nothing about us without us* (pp. 209–233). Policy.

EMCDDA (European Monitoring Centre for Drugs and Drug Addiction). (2020). *Problem drug use*. https://www.emcdda.europa.eu/topics/problem-drug-use_en

Kleiman, M. A., Caulkins, J. P., & Hawken, A. (2011). *Drugs and drug policy: What everyone needs to know*. Oxford University Press.

Leonard, J., & Windle, J. (2020). 'I could have went down a different path': Talking to people who used drugs problematically and service providers about Irish drug policy alternatives. *International Journal of Drug Policy, 84*, 102891.

Lynch, O. (2015). Desistance and de-radicalization—The case of terrorism and political violence. In S. Zeiger & A. Aly (Eds.), *Countering violent extremism: Developing an evidence base for policy and practice*. Curtin University Press.

Lynch, O., Windle, J., & Ahmed, Y. (2021). *Giving voice to diversity in criminological research: Nothing about us without us*. Policy.

Maruna, S. (2001). *Making good: How ex-convicts reform and rebuild their lives*. American Psychological Association Press.

Maruna, S., & Farrall, S. (2004). Desistance from crime: A theoretical reformulation. *Kolner Zeitschrift Fur Soziologie Und Sozialpsychologie, 43*(2), 171–194.

McNeill, F. (2016). Desistance and criminal justice in Scotland. In H. Croall, G. Mooney, & R. Munro (Eds.), *Crime, justice and society in Scotland* (pp. 200–216). Routledge.

McNeill, F., Farrall, S., Lightowler, C., & Maruna, S. (2012). *How and why people stop offending: Discovering desistance*. IRISS.

Pollak, S. (2017, February 2). More than 70% of prisoners have addiction issues, *Irish Times*.

Robinson, A., & Hamilton, P. (2016). *Moving on from crime and substance use: Transforming identities*. Policy Press.

Roeyen, S. V., Anderson, S., Vanderplasschen, W., Colman, C., & Vander Laenen, F. (2017). Desistance in drug-using offenders: A narrative review. *European Journal of Criminology, 14*(5), 606–625.

Sampson, R., & Laub, J. (1993). Crime and deviance in the life course. *Annual Review of Sociology, 18*(1), 63–84.

Weaver, B., & McNeill, F. (2007). *Giving up crime: Directions for policy*. Scottish Centre for Crime and Justice Research.

World Health Organisation. (2018). *Alcohol, drugs and addictive behaviours unit*. http://www.who.int/topics/substance_abuse/en/

CHAPTER 2

Desistance and Recovery in the Academic Literature

Abstract The link between addiction and offending is well established, however, the relationship is complex, and a range of causal models exist. This chapter explores the existing models that explain the relationship between addiction and offending and considers their relevance for a population of persistent offenders with multiple convictions. This chapter goes on to critique the literature on desistance and recovery examining issues of recidivism, and the relationship between the process of desistance and recovery from addiction. Finally, the chapter explores social identity, and psychological and narrative approaches to understanding desistance and recovery.

Keywords Addiction · Offending · Recidivism · Substance use

The link between drug misuse and crime has been described as 'one of the most reliable results obtainable in criminology' (Welte et al., 2001). For example, a review or meta-analysis of 30 studies exploring the drugs-crime link found the chance of offending is 3–4 times greater for people who use drugs than for people who do not use drugs, with the highest rates of offending among those in active addiction (Bennett et al., 2008). Still, the relationship between drugs and crime is complicated. Bennett

G. Cambridge et al., *The Desistance Journey*,
https://doi.org/10.1007/978-3-031-11269-0_2

and Holloway (2005: 76) have proposed that the complex relationship between drugs and crime can be split into four causal models:

(a) drug use causes crime, through either psychopharmacology or economic effects (i.e. people fight because they are intoxicated or steal because they need money for drugs),
(b) crime causes drug use (i.e. people take drugs because it is part of a criminal culture),
(c) the drug-crime relationship is bi-directional (i.e. we first use drugs because of our criminal activity, but consumption increases because of ongoing criminal activity), and
(d) there is a common cause (i.e. psychological and/or social factors cause both crime and drug use).

The last model is the most relevant for this book and arguably more appropriate overall. Research studies repeatedly show that high rates of both crime and problematic drug use are concentrated in areas suffering economic disadvantage and social disenfranchisement and exclusion (Stevens, 2011). A study conducted in Cork City by Leonard and Windle (2020: 4) supports this finding as participants reported using drugs to 'dull the pain of exclusion and lack of employment'.

As an explanatory framework, the causal model pointing to a combination of social and psychological issues is more appropriate given the life stories of the men recounted in this book. As will be discussed in later chapters, their experiences point to a complex transition into both offending and problematic drug use understood by the men as linked to neglect in childhood, trauma in the home and the community, lack of educational opportunity and broader social exclusion. These issues were exacerbated by what the men saw as the limitations of their community, notably the existence of what they call a 'hard-man' subculture that prioritised engaging in risk-taking behaviour, a willingness to use violence and, heavy drinking and drug use.

Regardless of causal links between drugs and crime, there is a strong evidence base showing that recidivism rates are higher for drug-using offenders (Colman et al., 2012). Schroeder and colleagues (2007: 193) argue that problematic drug use 'uniquely complicates desistance processes' partly by fracturing pro-social bonds (i.e. positive social relationships) (also Best, 2019). This issue of pro-social bonds is particularly important in this research, and for individuals working with people who use drugs who end up engaged with the criminal justice system. While drug use is not a *causal* feature in recidivism, it is a significant part of the story. Other risk factors for recidivism include poor educational attainment, a lack of pro-social role models (Schroeder et al., 2007), lack of employment and homelessness (Makarios et al., 2010). There are, however, further complications for drug-using offenders—notably that drug use/relapse and imprisonment are circular and, as such, drug use is predictive of a high recidivism rate and repeat imprisonment is a risk factor for relapse (see Graham, 2016). Furthermore, for drug-using individuals who go to prison, when attempting to desist or recover, a complex combination of structural, social and personal factors can impede their progress. For example, drug-using offenders often have chequered employment histories (Roeyen et al., 2017) and may carry various stigmas within their community long after recovery. This is yet another issue for the individual to deal with and overcome.

Rehabilitation from Addiction and Desistance from Crime as a Duel Process

As mentioned, the limited literature that comprehensively addresses the relationship between addiction and offending acknowledges that drug use (and lack of) has an impact on desistance from offending. Of the three studies identified by Roeyen and colleagues (2017) addressing recovery *and* desistance, all three found a positive direct relationship between substance abuse and offending, and all three argue that desistance from offending is subordinate to recovery from drug use (see Colman & Vander Laenen, 2012; Marsh, 2011; McCray et al., 2011); in other words, recovery from addiction comes before or above desisting from crime. While the literature on this duel process has grown somewhat in the five years since Roeyen and colleagues (2017) published their pessimistic review (see Chapters in Best & Colman, 2020; Robinson & Hamilton, 2016) this process remains under-researched, and not yet fully understood.

The literature, based upon self-report measures and interview data with people attempting to overcome addiction and offending, points out that the individuals see themselves in recovery rather than in a process of desistance. For them, stopping their involvement in crime is an outcome of their recovery from addiction. It is not a simple process to separate out the desistance and recovery journeys, however, as the process of recovery looks very much like desistance and vice versa. For example, both recovery and desistance processes prioritise the development of new social networks, both processes focus on how to build a more positive sense of self and re/construct an identity, and both processes focuses on personal growth and the development of empathy skills alongside engaging in psycho-education or education about the origins of their attitudes, feelings and behaviours (Roeyen et al., 2017; also Best, 2016; Irving, 2016).

While recovery and desistance frameworks advocate similar stages and processes they play out differently for every individual who engages because they are influenced by personogenic characteristics. Factors such as identity and the potential for identity shift are important for all desisters, but a new meaningful and positive personal identity is vital for people who have problematically used drugs as it allows them to comprehensively detach themselves from their 'addict' identity and reinvent themselves as a pro-social member of society (see Chapters in Robinson & Hamilton, 2016). For drug-using desisters, developing a sense of agency seems to be a vital part of the move through desistance and recovery. Roeyen and colleagues (2017) suggest that, in the limited research that exists in the field, it is important that drug-using offenders conceive of their journey as self-motivated. This is often portrayed as a response to having hit 'rock bottom' whereby choosing to recover and desist represents a deliberate and personal decision (also Irving, 2016).

Social Identity, Desistance and Recovery

It has long been recognised that most people mature out of crime. What has been called the age-crime curve suggests that offending peaks in the late teenage years and gradually declines thereafter. While this is true for most people, those from economically disadvantaged areas tend to have 'higher and wider' curves than those from more economically prosperous areas. Furthermore, some individuals, known as persisters, continue to engage in criminal activity long into adulthood; that is, desistance does not happen naturally for a small percentage of the *mature* population (Loeber & Farrington, 2012: 317). Maruna (2001: 34) has, however, called maturity a 'dangerously vague' concept that should only be used 'sparingly'. A desistance study by Coyle (2019) identified maturity as a series of rites of passage, such as 'completing education, entering full-time employment, getting married and becoming a parent', rather than simply hitting a certain age. Identifying maturity as rites of passage tied into structural processes, therefore, links maturation with other desistance theories rather than simply equating it to having reached adulthood.

It is increasingly recognised that desistance is not just about the individual, nor just about a process a person undertakes. It is about the opportunities the person is afforded to support them to desist and how they are received when they do desist (see Healy & O'Donnell, 2008; Maruna et al., 2004; McNeill, 2016; Farrell, 2019). Another issue, one which is also a limitation of the current study, is that most research participants are men, and there are significant differences in how women attempt to and are enabled (or not) to desist (see for example Seaman & Lynch, 2022a, 2022b).

Identity formation and reformation are key processes in both recovery and desistance (Shapland et al., 2016). But identity is not just about the individual, an individual's identity is not formed in isolation and is a reflection on their personal and interpersonal experiences as well as the values, norms and cultures that they adhere to. In other words, identity is social. Social identity, incorporating a sense of belonging, peer acceptance and identity acceptance or denial (Seaman & Lynch, 2016) are all important parts of the process of desistance and recovery—from the initial decision to commit to changing one's behaviour to the reintegration into a community and contributing to society (Giordano et al., 2007). The research attending to identity and identity change emerged in response to what was seen as the weaknesses of social control approaches to desistance and the opportunity reduction models of crime prevention (Laub & Sampson, 2003). These approaches focused on social learning, and socialisation processes as ways of addressing offending. While identity features as part of these approaches, they are only seen as having limited relevance (Giordano et al., 2007).

The early work of Maruna focused on identity and narratives and represented a sea-change in how we thought about crime, offending and desistance (Maruna, 2001; Maruna & Farrall, 2004; Maruna & Roy, 2007). Maruna and colleagues developed a theory of desistance where identity was central to the change process for individuals (also Healy, 2012, 2016; Healy & O'Donnell, 2008). For Maruna (2001), 'making good' is not about an absolute change in identity, but a reinterpretation of one's past offending behaviours to support the idea that an individual is fundamentally a good person who was waylaid (also Paternoster, et al., 2016). The focus of this work is based on the stories people tell themselves about who they are, what they were, how they reconcile and distance themselves from their past behaviour and how they can be a good person going forward.

Maruna emphasised the *scripts* that people drew upon to tell the story of who they are and were, with particular focus on the *redemptive* script. This script or story that the desisters tell about themselves demonstrates a fundamental optimism whereby they see themselves as a good person in a bad situation. The important thing was they saw hope in their future, because once the *bad situation* was resolved (e.g. poverty, abuse, peer pressure etc.), the good person they are (and were) would be allowed to emerge. The opposite of this redemptive script is a *condemnation script* where individuals feel no agency in their lives, cannot see a way out of their offending lifestyle and see themselves as destined to sustain their current lifestyle (Maruna, 2001; Maruna & Farrall, 2004; Maruna & Roy, 2007); in other words a fatalistic view on their situation. A shift from condemnation to a redemptive script is seen as an important development in the desistance journey, and for the individual, this means adopting a positive sense of self, a sense of agency over their own behaviour and a positive future-focused outlook on life.

While identity is clearly a part of desistance and recovery, as found in a range of desistance studies (e.g. Paternoster & Bushway, 2009; Paternoster et al., 2016), this book argues that, for desistance, identity and identity shift can only be understood when considered alongside community culture, meaning-making around drug taking, masculinity and addiction. As a means to bridge the social and shared meaning making nature of identity and its relevance to desistance, focusing on social identity has the capacity to make a useful contribution (Stets & Burk, 2000). The strength of focusing on social identity lies in the emphasis on the emergence of identity, not in isolation but through involvement in social groups, something we will return to when we discuss recovery processes. Social identity approaches, therefore, are founded upon a belief that individuals fundamentally seek positive self-images, but these are not just *internal* images but images dependent on the context which emerges from interpersonal and intergroup interactions. In other words, self-image depends on where we are, what is going on around us and who we interact with.

Social identity goes beyond self-image, it explains how we *organise* ourselves in society: we all define ourselves as part of the one or several groups we belong to (the in-group) and the groups we do not belong to (the out-group). The in-group (us) could include family, peer group, football club or nationality. The out-group (them) can be anyone outside these circles, such as people from other families, areas of the city, football clubs or nations. As individuals can and do shift identity groups, our perception of in/out-groups can change. This means, in the context of this study, it is not inconceivable for an individual to move from identifying with a drug-using peer group to identifying with a recovery focused peer group—and relatedly incorporate this identity into his sense of self (Kay & Monaghan, 2019).

While social identity approaches have been applied to the case of recovery from addiction, and despite recognition of the role these frameworks may have in explaining desistance, there has been little consideration of how social identity issues might apply directly to the issue of addiction and desistance as inseparable processes (Best, 2019; Kay & Monaghan, 2019). Two models from the social identity approach that have recently been proposed to explain recovery from addiction and addictive behaviours that seem to have relevance for desistance are the Social Identity Model of Cessation Maintenance (SIMCM) (Frings & Albery, 2015) and the Social Identity Model of Recovery (SIMOR) (Best et al., 2016; Kay & Monaghan, 2019).

The SIMCM proposes that individuals who are trying to abstain can support the development of their own emerging *non-drug* using identity by drawing on the social identities of individuals who had similar experiences and come through recovery (think secondary desistance). In a similar vein, SIMOR focuses on recovery as a process of identity change, where the individual's identity changes from *person who was dependant on drugs* to a *person in recovery*; but again these identities (i.e. drug user versus non-drug user) are scaffolded by support from recovery groups (e.g. Alcoholic/Narcotic Anonymous). Developing a new positive social identity can take time; during this process, the person is learning a new way to live their life with new values, norms, beliefs and attitudes. Time is often the key to this process and long-term engagement is important in the development of this new identity (Best et al., 2016). Existing programmes for individuals dealing with addiction embody the principles of longevity and prioritise social identity; programmes such as Alcoholics Anonymous (AA) and Narcotics Anonymous (NA) focus heavily on building new social connections in order to change ones self-definition and as a result impact social identity. Furthermore, as Best (2019: 38) notes, 12-step type programmes help people who had 'limited access to pro-social groups and networks' to find communal support and encouragement towards identity changes (also Irving, 2016; Marsh, 2011). While there are clear similarities between existing theories of desistance and SIMCM and SIMOR—notably the emphasis on building new pro-social identities and the need for community supports—the mechanisms that underpin these approaches have yet to be fully developed or explored.

Recovery and Desistance

It is often assumed that the processes of recovery and desistance have similar characteristics. While this is true in some cases, some research points to substantial differences between these processes (Best & Colman, 2020). Primary amongst these differences is the focus of the processes themselves: recovery is conceived as a personal journey of change, medicalised in many cases, and related to an improvement in an individual's quality of life. Desistance is conceived as a change resulting in socially desirable outcomes (i.e. crime prevention), forced through criminal justice responses, in many cases, less often focused upon the offenders quality of life. While this is a simplification of the two processes (Roeyen et al., 2017) there is some evidence of overlapping mechanisms that link recovery and desistance. The focus on negative turning points—often called 'rock bottom'—is one overlapping theme (i.e. Irving, 2016; Laub & Sampson, 2001). Both recovery and desistance frameworks incorporate the idea of suffering as a motivator for change (Carlsson, 2012; Chen, 2018), however, it is not known if this is a motivator or part of a narrative of change that a person constructs as they continue their personal journey. Objectively there is no way of knowing where or what turning points are, and for many individuals on a desistance or recovery journey, there are multiple turning points. This is something we will return to later. Finally, both desistance and recovery involve processes of identity change (Marsh, 2011), which are not linear but 'dynamic, gradual and subject to relapse' (Best & Colman, 2020: 3), and often involve a large number of professionals and peers supporting, or working with, individuals moving towards change (Graham, 2016).

A recent review of the literature on relationships between recovery and desistance points out that the overlaps and differences between the two processes are ill defined. It also found that, in the literature, there is an assumed relationship between recovery and desistance—that they are not mutually exclusive and in fact often occur simultaneously. There is, however, little detail provided as to the dynamics of the relationship nor how the processes proceed (Best et al., 2017). In addition, we know little about how individuals conceive of and experience these processes (or process). Furthermore, studies that address both recovery and desistance have tended to focus on categorising the processes, documenting risk and resilience factors, and identifying shared and divergent characteristics across processes.

While all of this is understandable given the conceptual immaturity of this area, this book aims to go some way towards overcoming this issue by examining how individuals on the journey to recovery and desistance see the processes. By conducting a Grounded Theory analysis of the life stories of 40 men who self-identify as experiencing addiction and participating in offending, this book seeks to understand if and how the process can be separated, how issues such as identity, culture and peer networks are relevant and how the individuals themselves understand recovery and desistance. Such analysis contributes a richness to discussions on desistance and recovery that ground their findings directly in the testimony of the participants. The voices of the participants are central to this work. The choice of this methodology was to ensure that rich data would inform the emergence of themes and theory and so contribute to our knowledge of the processes inherent in both recovery and desistance. The sample chosen for this study are from a particular geographic area in the south of Ireland and accurately represent both the diversity and the characteristic profile of individuals who are incarcerated in the local prison. The extremely high incidence of addiction amongst this population has greatly influenced the approach to desistance in this study. In short, this study, and the book it is based upon, add to the limited academic literature by exploring both desistance and rehabilitation, with a focus on the mechanics involved in both processes, and the narratives participants use to facilitate their pathways in and out of addiction and crime.

References

Bennett, T., & Holloway, K. (2005). *Understanding drugs, alcohol and crime.* McGraw-Hill.

Bennett, T., Holloway, K., & Farrington, D. (2008). The statistical association between drug misuse and crime: A meta-analysis. *Aggression and Violent Behaviour, 13*(2), 107–118.

Best, D. (2016). Social identity, social networks and social capital in desistance and recovery. In A. Robinson & Hamilton, P. (Eds.), *Moving on from crime and substance use: Transforming identities* (pp. 175–186). Policy Press.

Best, D. (2019). *Pathways to recovery and desistance.* Policy.

Best, D., & Colman, C. (2020). *Strengths-based approaches to crime and substance use: From drugs and crime to desistance and recovery.* Routledge.

Best, D., Beckwith, M., Haslam, S., Haslam, A., Jetten, J., Mawson, E., & Lubman, D. (2016). Overcoming alcohol and other drug addiction as a process of social identity transition: The social identity model of recovery (SIMOR). *Addiction Research and Theory, 24*(2), 111–123.

Best, D., Irving, J., & Albertson, K. (2017). Recovery and desistance: What the emerging recovery movement in the alcohol and drug area can learn from models of desistance from offending. *Addiction Theory and Research, 25*(1), 1–10.

Carlsson, C. (2012). Using 'turning points' to understand processes of change in offending: Notes from a Swedish study on life courses and crime. *The British Journal of Criminology, 52*(1), 1–16.

Chen, G. (2018). Building recovery capital: The role of hitting bottom in desistance and recovery from substance abuse and crime. *Journal of Psychoactive Drugs, 50*(5), 420–419.

Colman, C., & Vander Laenen, F. (2012). Recovery came first: Desistance versus recovery in the criminal careers of drug-using offenders. *The Scientific World Journal, 2012*, 1–9. |Article ID 657671 | https://doi.org/10.1100/2012/657671

Coyle, B. (2019). 'What the f** k Is Maturity?': Young adulthood, subjective maturity and desistance from crime. *The British Journal of Criminology, 59*(5), 1178–1198.

Farrell, S. (2019). The architecture of desistance. Routledge.

Frings, D., & Albery, I. P. (2015). The social identity model of cessation maintenance: Formulation and initial evidence. *Addictive Behaviors, 44*(1), 35–42.

Giordano, P. C., Schroeder, R. D., & Cernkovich, S. A. (2007). Emotions and crime over the life course: A neo-Meadian perspective on criminal continuity and change. *American Journal of Sociology, 112*(6), 1603–1661.

Graham, H. (2016). *Rehabilitation work: Supporting desistance and recovery.* Routledge.

Healy, D. (2012). *The dynamics of desistance: Charting pathways through change*. Routledge.

Healy, D. (2016). 'I've always tried but I hadn't got the willpower': Understanding pathways to desistance in the Republic of Ireland. In J. Shapland, S. Farrall, & A. Bottoms (Eds.), *Global perspectives on desistance: Reviewing what we know and looking to the future* (pp. 50–65). Routledge.

Healy, D., & O'Donnell, I. (2008). Calling time on crime: Motivation, generativity and agency in Irish probationers. *Probation Journal, 55*(1), 25–38.

Irving, J. (2016). Alcoholics anonymous: Sustaining behavioural change. In A. Robinson & P. Hamilton (Eds.), *Moving on from crime and substance use: Transforming identities*. Policy.

Kay, C., & Monaghan, M. (2019). Rethinking recovery and desistance processes: Developing a social identity model of transition. *Addiction Research and Theory, 27*(1), 47–54.

Laub, J. H., & Sampson, R. J. (2001). Understanding desistance from crime. *Crime and Justice, 28*(1), 1–69.

Laub, J. H., & Sampson, R. J. (2003). *Shared beginnings, divergent lives: Delinquent boys to age 70*. Harvard University Press.

Leonard, J., & Windle, J. (2020). 'I could have went down a different path': Talking to people who used drugs problematically and service providers about Irish drug policy alternatives. *International Journal of Drug Policy, 84*, 102891.

Loeber, R., & Farrington, D. P. (2012). *From Juvenile delinquency to adult crime: Criminal careers, justice policy, and prevention*. Oxford University Press.

Makarios, M., Steiner, B., & Travis, L. F. (2010). Examining the predictors of recidivism among men and women released from prison in Ohio. *Criminal Justice and Behavior, 37*(12), 1377–1391.

Marsh, B. (2011). Narrating desistance: Identity change and the 12-step script. *Irish Probation Journal, 8*(1), 49–68.

Maruna, S. (2001). *Making good: How ex-convicts reform and rebuild their lives*. American Psychological Association Press.

Maruna, S., & Farrall, S. (2004). Desistance from crime: A theoretical reformulation. *Kolner Zeitschrift Fur Soziologie Und Sozialpsychologie, 43*(2), 171–194.

Maruna, S., & Roy, K. (2007). Amputation or reconstruction? Notes on 'knifing off' and desistance from crime. *Journal of Contemporary Criminal Justice, 23*(1), 104–124.

Maruna, S., Lebel, T. P., Mitchell, N., & Naples, M. (2004). Pygmalion in the reintegration process: Desistance from crime through the looking glass. *Psychology, Crime and Law, 10*(3), 271–281.

McCray, K., Wesely, J. K., & Rasche, C. E. (2011). Rehab retrospect: Former prostitutes and the (re)construction of deviance. *Deviant Behavior, 32*(8), 743–768.

McNeill, F. (2016). Desistance and criminal justice in Scotland. In H. Croall, G. Mooney, & R. Munro (Eds.), *Crime, justice and society in Scotland* (pp. 200–216). Routledge.

Paternoster, R., & Bushway, S. (2009). Desistance and the "feared self": Toward an identity theory of criminal desistance. *The Journal of Criminal Law and Criminology, 99*(3), 1103–1156.

Paternoster, R., Bachman, R., Kerrison, E., O'Connell, D., & Smith, L. (2016). Desistance from crime and identity: An empirical test with survival time. *Criminal Justice and Behaviour, 43*(9), 1204–1224.

Robinson, A., & Hamilton, P. (2016). *Moving on from crime and substance use: Transforming identities*. Policy Press.

Roeyen, S. V., Anderson, S., Vanderplasschen, W., Colman, C., & Vander Laenen, F. (2017). Desistance in drug-using offenders: A narrative review. *European Journal of Criminology, 14*(5), 606–625.

Schroeder, R. D., Giordano, P. C., & Cernkovich, S. A. (2007). Drug use and desistance processes. *Criminology, 45*(10), 191–198.

Seaman, V., & Lynch, O. (2016). Learning the basics of how to live: Ex-prisoners accounts of doing desistance. *Irish Probation Journal, 16*(1), 65–83.

Seaman, V., & Lynch, O. (2022a). Knifing off? Social networks and the inadequacies of desistance frameworks for women in the criminal justice system in Ireland. In S. Grace, M. O'Neill, T. Walker, H. King, L. Baldwin, A. Jobe, O. Lynch, F. Measham, K. O'Brien, & V. Seaman (Eds.), *Criminal women; Gender matters* (pp. 20–35). Policy.

Seaman, V., & Lynch, O. (2022b). Perpetrators and victims: Women, double deviance, and the criminal justice system. In I. Masson & N. Booth (Eds.), *Handbook of women's experiences in criminal justice*. Routledge.

Shapland, J., Farrall, S., & Bottoms, A. (2016). *Global perspectives on desistance*. Routledge.

Stets, J. E., & Burke, P. J. (2000). Identity theory and social identity theory. *Social Psychology Quarterly, 11*(2), 224–237.

Stevens, A. (2011). *Drugs, crime and public health: The political economy of drug policy*. Routledge.

Welte, J. W., Zhang, L., & Wieczorek, W. F. (2001). The effects of substance use on specific types of criminal offending in young men. *Journal of Research in Crime and Delinquency, 38*(4), 416–438.

CHAPTER 3

Cork City: Understanding the Context

Abstract This chapter provides the context to a study conducted in Cork City with city residents. It examines the geography, economic, social and educational landscape as relevant to this study and traces the impact of micro and macro-economic shocks on deprived communities across generations. The chapter outlines how housing policy, the presence and withdrawal of local industry and precarious employment impact the social mobility and stagnation of segments of the city population and how recovery from economic shocks is not evenly distributed across communities in the area. Finally, the chapter addresses social deprivation and drug use in Cork city.

Keywords Cork · Socio-economic status · Deprivation · Unemployment

Cork city is a medium-sized city by European standards with a population of just over 200,000 people, situated in the south of Ireland; it is the second largest city in the Republic of Ireland. There are substantial differences in the socio-economic profile of areas across the city but a useful indicter of the experience of disadvantage is the inclusion of an area in the Revitalising Areas by Planning, Investment and Development (RAPID) programme. Regions are included in a government programme where local government and local communities create a shared plan for

G. Cambridge et al., *The Desistance Journey*,
https://doi.org/10.1007/978-3-031-11269-0_3

regeneration. There are four designated RAPID Areas within Cork City, and these areas are home to 23 percent of the city's population:

- Knochnaheeney/Hollyhill/Churchfield
- Blackpool/the Glen/Mayfield
- Fairhill/Gurranabraher/Franree
- Togher/Mahon/Ballyphehane.

The areas of the city that are the focus of this study are designated RAPID areas. The most recent socio-economic profile of the city by Cork City Council (2020) noted the areas as being disadvantaged or very disadvantaged and, having a low participation rate in third-level education, a relatively high population under age 18, a high percentage of social housing, a low labour force participation rate and high unemployment rate. These RAPID areas have long histories of state neglect and under-investment.

The experience of un/underemployed youth in the RAPID areas today can be mapped onto their parents and grandparents experiences over a forty year period. For example, in the 1970s working-class employment was plentiful and by the 1980s nearly 75 percent of working age males were employed outside of family businesses. However, the Irish working classes suffered low-levels of upward mobility and by the late 1980s, 70 percent of working-class men were the children of working-class parents (Crowley et al., 2005).

This is partially due to a situation that was witnessed in other countries, where many key industries collapsed during the 1980s due to a combination of deindustrialisation and global economic downturn. This downturn hit Cork hard with major unemployment experienced due to the closure of two international manufacturing plants in the City; Fords and Dunlops. The closure of these companies had tragic consequences for those living in Cork's working-class neighbourhoods, many of which feature in today's RAPID programme. The impact of the global recession in the 1980s was exacerbated by local decisions to invest in more affluent middle-class areas leading to a very striking division of the city along economic lines. This division was evidenced in housing provision, educational attainment, employment, but also linked to the failure of the disadvantaged areas to benefit from any furture upturn in the economy.

The housing situation in Cork mirrored the growth of industry in the 1970s and cheap prefabricated housing was rapidly built to meet the demand of industrial workers. These housing schemes were built in what are now RAPID areas of the city. The prefabricated method had a short life cycle and led to a constant need for upgrading and renovation (O'Connell, 2007; also Committee Report, 1979). These schemes and others built in the 1980s were socially, geographically and economically isolated and, unemployment and social problems became endemic to these areas (Hourihan, 1979).

A large percentage of residents of these local authority housing estates worked in Cork's main industries—the Ford car plant, the Dunlop tyre company, as well as the dockyards, and the residents of these estates were badly impacted by the collapse of these industries in the 1980s: many households became reliant on state aid for the long-term. To make matters worse, the Government introduced the Tenancy Surrender Grant in 1984 whereby residents in social housing units were paid to relocate to these new estates. As many of these individuals were unemployed and in receipt of social welfare payments (O'Connell, 2007), this added to the cycle of poverty that already existed in the area. These policies clustered individuals experiencing poverty and social exclusion into a small number of mostly Northside estates. Ultimately, the social housing provided in Cork City, particularly that constructed in the Northside, was developed with little thought for the industrial potential of the area (Brunt, 1988) nor any planning around maintenance, social facilities or community development. Residents still suffer the consequences of these decisions today.

The Good Times—for Some

The prolonged recession of the 1980s and early 1990s was followed by the so-called Celtic Tiger era when the country witnessed rapid economic growth from 1995 until approximately 2008. Quite expectedly economic boom and bust was not experienced in the same manner by all the residents of Cork City.

While social mobility increased for some during this period (McWilliams, 2005) prosperity was not evenly distributed throughout Irish society. In Cork, as in the rest of Ireland, rocketing house prices locked many working-class families out of the housing market, particularly in urban areas. Local authority housing became the only option for some (Allen, 2000) at a time when social housing stock was declining. Working class employment also became unstable, with precarious employment becoming the norm (Healy & Reynolds, 1990). Consequently, levels of both absolute and relative poverty increased (Kirby, 2002), as did the divide between rich and poor (Allen, 2000); this led to the growth of the so-called 'underclass' of welfare-dependent families (Ilan, 2015).

The Celtic Tiger economic boom had ended by 2008 when the world entered the Great Recession. Between 2008 and 2011 Ireland's national income dropped by over 10 percent (Callan et al., 2013) and Ireland moved from having the second lowest rate of unemployment in Europe, to having the second highest (White, 2010). Unemployment peaked at 15 percent in 2012, with youth unemployment peaking at 33 percent (Kelly & McGuinness, 2015). The 2008 recession led to a threefold increase in unemployment in Cork between 2005 and 2011, and the number of people receiving social welfare payments increased from 9616 (2005) to over 26,000 (2010). In one RAPID area, 43.3 percent of adults were out of work at the height of the recession in 2010 (CSO, 2011).

By 2016, as Ireland emerged from the Great Recession, the number of people receiving social welfare payments had fallen to 8,943, or 8.3 percent of the population. Six Northside estates were however still deemed 'unemployment black spots' because the proportion of unemployment was greater than 35 percent. That these areas also possessed the highest unemployment rates in 2011 (CSO, 2016) showed how little had changed. All six estates remained designated RAPID areas characterised by high numbers of local authority housing, low educational attainment and families with high numbers of children. Poor physical health was also above the national average (Kelly & Hayes, 2014). In short, economic deprivation, and all its related issues, have consistently been concentrated in those areas of the city which were shoddily and haphazardly built during the 1970s to house individuals working in industries which shuttered in the 1980s.

The Usual Suspects

Problematic drug use and crime are disproportionately concentrated in the RAPID areas of Cork City and these areas are where the majority of the 40 men who participated in this study grew up. This is perhaps no surprise because there is substantial evidence in the academic literature of the relationship between economic disadvantage and social exclusion and the likelihood of spending time in prison (IPRT, 2012). There is a long history of Irish research on this phenomenon. For example, in 1967, a survey of boys incarcerated in St Patricks Institution in Dublin found that inmates tended to come from large families in poor urban areas, with poor educational attainment, and their fathers were mostly unskilled or semi-skilled workers (Flynn et al., 1967). These findings were replicated three years later by the Kennedy Report (1970) and again over thirty years later by the Department of Justice, Equality and Law Reform, which reported that 80 percent of young people who came before the Dublin Children's Court lived in local authority housing (Kilkelly, 2006).

Similar results have been found in studies of the adult prison population. A study of Mountjoy (Dublin) prison inmates highlighted the prevalence of socio-economic disadvantage within the prison population: the majority of prisoners were from large families living in a small number of economically disadvantaged areas. If they had a job, they worked in poor-paying jobs and often they were unemployed, and most left school at the age of fourteen or earlier. The prisoners usually received their first conviction at the age of sixteen and many had spent time in juvenile detention (O'Mahony, 1997).

The concentration of the prison population from a small number of economically disadvantaged areas has been echoed by a number of more contemporary Irish studies (see Bacik & O'Connell, 1998; Hourigan, 2011; Kilkelly, 2006; Martynowicz & Quigley, 2010; O'Donnell et al., 2007; O'Mahony, 2003). Most of these studies highlight that those in custody not only experience economic deprivation, but family breakdown, school problems and substance abuse (Killkelly, 2006). For example, Griffin and Kelleher (2010) interviewed a group of young men living in Limerick's most disadvantaged communities who were involved in crime. The fact that the men left school with no qualifications mostly excluded many from the labour market, so they had little structure to their day and, exhibited a sense of nihilism and hopelessness.

Only one small study has been undertaken on the links between economic deprivation and crime in Cork. Twenty years ago, Phillips (2002) interviewed people participating in the Intensive Probation Scheme in Cork City. The Scheme was set up to supervise offenders in the community instead of sending them to prison. All selected participants were persistent and serious offenders originating from Cork: sixty percent had left school without any qualifications, and only one percent had completed the leaving cert (Ireland's final secondary education exam).

While 59 percent of participants had been employed at some stage in their lives, the majority of their work was casual and manual-unskilled. Some 41 percent reported having never been employed and 62 percent came from Northside housing estates. In this study, the average age of first conviction for the boys was 16 years and the first prison sentence commenced at 18 years.

Conclusion

This chapter is not suggesting that all of those living in Cork's working-class communities engage in offending, nor that a propensity for offending emerges from these communities, but rather points out that those who ultimately engage in problematic drug use and crime very often experience significant disadvantage, and while crime is high in these communities so is victimhood. Importantly, the conditions that have given rise to this disadvantage, particularly Cork's experience of geographically concentrated economic deprivation and inequality, dovetail with experiences documented in cities from Glasgow, London and Oxford (Hobbs, 2001; McLean, 2019; Windle, 2021) to Philadelphia and New York (Anderson, 1999; Bourgois, 1995). The similarities across contexts point to the importance influence of structural conditions on an individual's experience, behaviour, potential and progress. While addiction and crime may be often told of as deficits of the person in public narratives, the reality is that the conditions that give rise to high rates of addiction and offending cannot and should not be dismissed.

References

Allen, K. (2000). *The celtic tiger: The myth of social partnership*. Manchester University Press.

Anderson, E. (1999). *Code of the street: Decency, violence, and the moral life of the inner city*. Norton.

Bacik, I., & O'Connell, M. (1998). *Crime and poverty in Ireland*. Round Hall.

Bourgois, P. (1995). *In search of respect: Selling crack in El Barrio*. Cambridge University Press.

Brunt, B. (1988). The new industrialization of Ireland. In R. Carter & A. J. Parker (Eds.), *Ireland: A contemporary geographical perspective* (pp. 115–131). Routledge.

Callan, T., Nolan, B., Keane, C., Savage, M., & Walsh, J. (2013). The great recession, austerity and inequality: Evidence from Ireland. *Intereconomics, 48*(6), 335–338.

Committee Report (1979). *Letter to clerk to joint committee from Cork corporation.* Available from: http://archive.oireachtas.ie/1980/APPENDIX_02101980_6.html

Cork City Council (2020). *Cork City socio-economic summary profile.* Online at https://www.corkcity.ie/en/media-folder/cork-city-development-plan/socio-economic-summary-profile.pdf

Crowley, J., Devoy, R., Linehan, D., & O'Flanagan, P. (2005). *Atlas of Cork City.* Cork University Press.

CSO (Central Statistics Office). (2011). *This is Ireland, census 2011.* Available at: http://www.cso.ie/en/census/census2011reports/census2011thisisirelandpart1/

CSO (Central Statistics Office). (2016). *This is Ireland, census 2016.* Available at: https://www.cso.ie/en/census/census2016reports/

Flynn, A., McDonald, N., & O'Doherty, F. (1967). A survey of boys in St. *Patrick's Institution, Irish Jurist, 2*(1), 222–232.

Griffin, M., & Kelleher, P. (2010). Uncertain futures: Men on the margins in Limerick City. *Irish Probation Journal, 7*(1), 24–46.

Healy, S., & Reynolds, B. (1990). *Work, unemployment and job-creation policy.* CORI Justice Commission.

Hobbs, D. (2001). The firm. Organizational logic and criminal culture on a shifting terrain. *British Journal of Criminology, 41*(4), 549–560.

Hourigan, N. (2011). *Understanding limerick.* Cork University Press.

Hourihan, K. (1979). The cork land use and transportation study. *Irish Geography, 12*(1), 99–104.

Ilan, J. (2015). *Understanding street culture: Poverty, crime, youth and cool.* Macmillan.

IPRT (Irish Penal Reform Trust) (2012). *The vicious circle of social exclusion and crime.* Online at https://www.iprt.ie/site/assets/files/6264/position_paper_final.pdf

Kelly, E., & McGuinness, S. (2015). Impact of the Great Recession on unemployed and NEET individuals' labour market transitions in Ireland. *Economic Systems, 39*(1), 59–71.

Kelly, T., & Hayes, P. (2014). *Cork City profile. A statistical and Geographical profile of Cork City local authority area focused on health and social inclusion.* Cork Healthy Cities and Social Inclusion Unit.

Kennedy Report. (1970). *Reformatory and industrial schools systems report.* The Stationary Office.

Kilkelly, U. (2006). Operationalising children's rights: Lessons from research. *Journal of Children's Services, 1*(4), 35–46.

Kirby, P. (2002). *Reinventing Ireland*. Pluto.
Martynowicz, A., & Quigley, M. (2010). *It's like stepping on a landmine...—reintegration of prisoners in Ireland*. Irish Penal Reform Trust.
McLean, R. (2019). *Gangs, drugs and (dis) organised crime*. Policy.
McWilliams, D. (2005). *The pope's children*. Gill.
O'Connell, C. (2007). *The state and housing in Ireland: Ideology, policy and practice*. Nova Science.
O'Donnell, I., Teljeur, C., Hughes, N., Baumer, E., & Kelly, A. (2007). When prisoners go home: Punishment, social deprivation and the geography of reintegration. *Irish Criminal Law Journal, 17*(4), 3–9.
O'Mahony, P. (1997). *Mountjoy prisoners: A sociological and criminological profile*. The Stationery Office.
O'Mahony, P. (2003). *Criminal justice in Ireland*. Institute of Public Administration.
Phillips, G. (2002). *An empirical study of the intensive probation scheme in Cork: Incorporating a qualitative and longitudinal analysis*. MA thesis: University College Cork.
White, T. J. (2010). Celtic collapse, or Celtic correction? Ireland's recession in historical perspective. *New Hibernia Review, 14*(4), 27–43.
Windle, J. (2021). Reconsidering the 1991 Blackbird Leys Rioters as an underclass: an insider perspective. In O. Lynch, J. Windle, & Y. Ahmed (Eds.) *Giving voice to diversity in criminological research: Nothing about us without us* (pp. 133–148). Policy.

CHAPTER 4

Methodology

Abstract This chapter outlines the data collection and analysis processes carried out for this study. The details of participants are documented, the analysis method, Grounded Theory, is discussed and Life History Criminology, the basis for the data analysis, is reviewed. A detailed discussion around recruitment, insider-research and best practice in research with vulnerable populations is presented and the personal account of the researchers is included. Finally, the details of the ethics permission process engaged with as part of this study are recounted.

Keywords Insider-research · Life histories · Grounded theory · Ethics

The study is concerned with understanding the life histories as recounted by men who had at one time in their lives come into contact with the criminal justice system. All 40 participants are from Cork, had been addicted (self defined) to alcohol and/or drugs in the past and have criminal records; most spent time in prison. A modified Grounded Theory approach (Charmaz, 2006) guided data collection and analysis. Semi-structured interviews were used to gain an understanding of these men's experiences. All interviews were conducted by the first author (Graham Cambridge) and his experiences are included in this chapter in italics and in the first person to illuminate the story of how the research was

G. Cambridge et al., *The Desistance Journey*,
https://doi.org/10.1007/978-3-031-11269-0_4

conducted. As an insider researcher—being from the area and working with individuals with similar histories to the participants in this study—his accounts reflect his insider status and how this was helpful during data collection. In addition, Graham reflects on how his own experience as a local practitioner/researcher from the Northside of the city was looked upon positively by the men—and how in some cases the participants saw him as a realistic and positive role model.

Modified Grounded Theory

The data collected for this study amassed to almost 80 hours of recorded interviews, and almost 1000 pages of text. In order to analyse this data, a means of organising and coding the data was needed. A popular software programme called Nvivo was used to organise the data and simplify record keeping. A modified Grounded Theory approach was chosen as the most appropriate method to analyse the content in the data. This method of analysis allows the researcher to identify themes across the data and allows the data to *speak for itself*—i.e. closely links the themes to the words of the men who participated. Grounded theory was appropriate for this study because the topic is a fundamentally understudied area. While desistance is widely researched in Ireland (i.e. Healy, 2012, 2016; Healy & O'Donnell, 2008; Seaman & Lynch, 2016), when this project commenced there were no studies of desistance in Cork city nor studies of the Cork prison population (although see Mulcahy, 2021). As such, it was unclear at the outset how desistance as a descriptive notion and a theoretical body of work might apply to a population sample from Cork city. Grounded theory is most useful for studies such as this one because the aim is to develop a theory on the relationship between experiences, addiction and offending. The study was not interested in simply describing the life histories of the men, but sought to discover the relationship between elements of their lives and experiences.

Charmaz (2006) argues that Grounded Theory should be seen as a set of principles and tools focusing on appreciating the process, and stresses the importance of action and the role of constructivism in understanding society for those being studied. Charmaz's approach was embraced in this study because of the understudied nature of the topic, and because it enabled the gathering of rich data, allowed for flexibility of data collection methods, and gave the researcher access to the participants' world: not only to descriptive accounts of their lives but also to the processes and challenges they faced in trying to change their lives. In short, it allowed us to learn how the men made sense of their lives. This enabled us to develop an analytic understanding of their meaning making and actions linked to this.

Life History Criminology

Semi-structured interviews were undertaken with 40 participants. The participants were all individuals who were accessed via gatekeeper organisations or using a snowballing (friends of friends) technique. The only criteria for involvement were having engagement with the criminal justice system in the past and being over 18 (see below). The interviews were organised around very general themes in order to elicit in-depth and contextualised life histories; general questions were prepared in advance but the interview only loosely followed a structure. In other words, the men were allowed to dictate the direction of the interview. Life history interviews have long been used to study criminal careers, beginning with Clifford Shaw's (1930) *The Jack Roller* and Edwin Sutherlands (1937) *The Professional Thief*. Sampson and Laub (1993: 204) highlight how 'the power of life-history data' is that it can 'illuminate the complex processes of criminal offending'. They are also critical of Criminology's traditional focus on 'the teenage years' and neglect of 'the link between early childhood behaviours and later adult outcomes' (Sampson & Laub, 1993: 6). Life course criminology links childhood and adulthood into the criminological picture by looking at the entire life span, while examining the different factors that correlate with the onset, persistence and desistance of criminal involvement over the individual's life.

During the last decade, there has been an upsurge in interest in narrative approaches to criminology (Maruna & Liem, 2021). This approach, pioneered by scholars such as Maruna (2001), McAdams (2001) and Presser (2009) asks 'what do stories do for their tellers and their listeners, why some stories are told and others untold, and how this telling impacts' behaviour' (Maruna & Liem, 2021: 126). In other words, self-narratives help people explain their actions and decipher their motivations (Marsh, 2011). All of us have life stories or narratives that inform who we are and how we represent ourselves. In this study, accessing the men's life history narratives enabled us to fully understand how they saw their experiences and how they recall and frame the processes of change they experienced. The interviews allowed us to explore the participant's life experiences and document their relationships with parents, siblings and peers, their educational and employment experiences, their contact with the criminal justice system, their drug use and delve into the difficulties encountered in desisting from crime and/or recovering from addiction. This approach focused not on the factual description or recall of the individual's life experiences, but on the processes, the interactivities, the interpersonal relationships and the developmental context of their life events, especially how the men understood the experiences and how they fit in with their overall story.

Access and Methods of Recruitment

The participants who took part of this study were initially recruited via posters placed in the organisation offices in Cork City (see below). The posters asked the potential participants to discuss the research with their case workers to see if it might be appropriate for them.

- The Cork Learning Support Service, who provides a range of educational programmes;
- The Cork Alliance Centre, who works with people released from prison and living in the Cork area;
- The Cork Local Drug Task Force, who meets the needs of individuals with substance abuse issues.

Snowball sampling (friends of friends) was then used to recruit further participants. Participants recruited through the three gatekeeper organisations recommended friends, family and acquaintances who might be interested in participating. When a recommendation was made, participants were asked to give the researcher's contact details to their friend/family member so they could choose to contact the researcher directly or not. Individuals who contacted the researcher in this way were all asked if they were a part of a support organisation, and if so, were asked to discuss participation with their case worker prior to involvement. All participants were involved with either a statutory group or NGO or both.

The poster stated that participants who had at one time or another been in contact with the criminal justice system were welcome to get involved. There was no requirement that the participants were male, had used drugs problematically, self-defined as addicts or had been to prison. The only limiting criteria were that they could not have been a client of the interviewer and were aged over 18 years old. That all participants self-defined as *addicts* was an unintended outcome of the sample chosen. The interviews for this study were conducted in person, in the local University buildings. All interviews were recorded on a digital device, transcribed as soon as possible after the interview and processed in Nvivo. Once transcribed the digital file was deleted.

Sample

Forty participants were interviewed and the first author was interviewed to saturation. That is, recruitment to the study ceased when new participants were no longer providing new insights (Charmaz, 2006). All participants were male and aged between 18 and 49 years old (under 18s were not accepted). Thirty-one participants came from the Northside of Cork City, eight came from the Southside of Cork City and one grew up in Limerick before moving to Cork. Participants were invited for interviews based on their history of engagement with the criminal justice system, or having been in prison. All but one of the participants had spent time in prison (Table 4.1).

All 40 of the men had self-defined issues with addiction to drugs and/or alcohol. All engaged at one point with outpatient addiction services and 21 had attended residential drug treatment centres: 12 attended more than one residential treatment intervention. Measuring desistance is more difficult than measuring recovery: all participants reported having stopped consuming alcohol and illicit drugs. While a difficulty with desistance research is knowing what counts as an absence of offending, Farrington (2007) has suggested that desistance researchers should focus on people who cease engaging in more serious crimes, rather than a total absence of offending. All participants in the current study reported that they were trying to lead what they described as an honest life.

Researcher Involvement

This research project was inspired by the first author's experience with, and interest in, the life histories of men who have come into contact with the criminal justice system in Cork. Graham has been working in the community since 2007 as a volunteer and later paid worker. He

Table 4.1 Participant demographics drawn from interview data

Participant	*From RAPID area of Cork City*	*Early school leaver*	*Had spent time in prison*	*Age at interview*	*Age of recovery*	*Recovery attempts*
P1	Yes	Yes	No	22	22	1+
P2	Yes	Yes	No	20	20	1+
P3	Yes	Yes	Yes	18	18	1+
P4	Yes	Yes	No	18	18	1+
P5	Yes	Yes	Yes	19	18	1+
P6	Yes	Yes	No	19	17	1+
P7	Yes	Yes	No	22	19	1+
P8	Yes	Yes	No	37	21	1+
P9	Yes	No	No	31	22	1+
P10	Yes	Yes	Yes	40	36	1+
P12	No	Yes	Yes	40	32	1+
P13	Yes	Yes	Yes	37	40	1+
P14	Yes	Yes	Yes	43	44	1+
P15	Yes	No	Yes	44	28	1+
P16	Yes	Yes	No	33	30	1+
P17	Yes	Yes	Yes	30	35	1+
P18	Yes	Yes	Yes	32	35	1+
P19	Yes	Yes	No	37	21	1+
P20	Yes	Yes	Yes	22	33	1+
P21	Yes	Yes	Yes	27	25	1+
P23	Yes	Yes	No	32	35	1+
P24	Yes	Yes	Yes	20	33	1+
P25	Yes	No	No	43	27	1+
P26	Yes	Yes	Yes	34	26	1+
P27	Yes	Yes	Yes	32	20	1+
P28	Yes	Yes	Yes	33	40	1+
P29	Yes	No	No	40	33	1+
P30	Yes	Yes	Yes	45	22	1+
P31	Yes	Yes	Yes	45	31	1+
P32	Yes	Yes	Yes	37	32	1+
P33	Yes	Yes	Yes	36	28	1+
P34	Yes	Yes	Yes	35	30	1+
P35	Yes	No	No	29	29	1+
P36	Yes	Yes	Yes	28	43	1+
P37	Yes	Yes	No	34	24	1+

(continued)

Table 4.1 (continued)

Participant	*From RAPID area of Cork City*	*Early school leaver*	*Had spent time in prison*	*Age at interview*	*Age of recovery*	*Recovery attempts*
P38	No	Yes	Yes	35	33	1
P39	Yes	Yes	Yes	43	35	1+
P40	Yes	No	Yes	26	49	1+

is currently employed as an outreach worker in a community organisation in Cork City. The organisation is funded predominantly by the Irish Probation Service, although his role is funded through the Health Service Executive in order to provide outreach support to people with addiction issues. The majority of the people on the outreach programme have recently been released from prison or are clients of the Irish Probation Service, although clients occasionally self-refer or are referred by other community organisations or treatment centres. While Graham did not interview any of his clients or former clients, most participants knew of his outreach work. We acknowledge that this may have impacted their interaction with him during the data collection process. The text in italics throughout the remainder of this section is a reflective piece, written in Graham's own words.

I was concerned with both doing no harm during this process and most importantly adding some benefit to the participant's lives. Life narrative research can have a beneficial even therapeutic value for participants, helping them look at their lives and can support them to face issues without the emotional component being central to the interaction. In this study, engaging participants via *service providers (i.e. gatekeepers) meant that participants were supported in their choice to engage with this research with appropriate services on hand if needed. Moreover, having come from the Northside and having accessed education as a mature student myself, I knew that few participants would have visited University College Cork, nor known anyone who attended the University. As such, I wanted to take the opportunity to bring the men to the University and expose them to the experience of being in that environment. I was cognisant of balancing the quite difficult experience of recounting their life experiences with a new and more positive experience of the potential for engaging in education and their inclusion in a university community they might have previously been (or perceived to have been) excluded from. In short, not only did I want to avoid causing harm but hoped that the overall experience of engaging in this study was positive, and might open some participants minds to the possibility of further education. Ultimately I succeeded in this aim as some of the men have since graduated with third levels qualifications, one of whom made the application to study whilst we were doing his life history interview for this study.*

During interviews I was aware of the trust the participants demonstrated towards me when they began telling their life-stories. They did not hold back when describing traumatic life experiences and sharing intimate information about their lives. The majority of the men provided detailed accounts of the difficulties they faced growing up in poverty and within dysfunctional family homes. Some went into great detail about the abuse they suffered as children and, how they felt and dealt with these devastating experiences.

I credit this trust and subsequent sharing to the experience I gained through my work as a support/outreach worker. Part of my role is to listen to people telling me about their difficult life experiences, and how these experiences affect them. I am also a qualified BSOC Youth and Community Worker. My education, employment and volunteer experience greatly assisted me in interviewing participants and gave me an advantage in gathering rich data: participants may have been less open in other circumstances.

I also had the added advantage of originating from the Northside of Cork City. This insider status not only enabled me to relate to the struggles the men faced growing up in disadvantaged areas of Cork city but also afforded me credibility as having a genuine interest in their story and potentially an understanding of where they were coming from. The participants knew I could empathise with their experiences. In short, my insider status gave the research validity (see Coghlan, 2003*;* Rooney, 2005*).*

Insider-research describes a range of situations whereby the researcher has a common connection or involvement with the research setting. This usually means they share an identity, first-hand knowledge and language with the people they are researching with (Asselin, 2003; see Windle, 2021). Bonner and Tolhurst (2002) recognised three key advantages of being an insider researcher:

1. Insiders have a better understanding of the culture being studied;
2. Insiders do not change the flow of social communication unnaturally;

3. Insiders have a reputable intimacy that encourages both the telling and the judging of truth.

Insider-researchers also have a pre-existing awareness of the environment of the research (Bell, 2005) and understand the politics of the society, including an understanding of the formal hierarchies and appreciation of how things 'really work'. In general, insiders have a great deal of knowledge, which takes an outsider a long time to acquire (Smyth & Holian, 2008; see Leonard & Windle, 2020; Windle, 2021).

During interviews, insider-researchers can 'ask meaningful questions and read non-verbal cues' while possessing the ability to 'project a more truthful, authentic understanding of the culture under study' (Merriam et al., 2001: 411). Interaction between participants and insider-researchers can be more natural and, can lessen the likelihood of researchers passing judgement or stereotype the participants in the research (Aguiler, 1981). Gaining access to participants can also be easier for insider-researchers (Chavez, 2008) as they know how to approach participants, who may be more inclined to talk to someone who understands them (Bell, 2005). Indeed, Bourgois (1995: 12) notes how it can be hard for drug users who come from already marginalised groups to trust academics and, as such, they may be slow to reveal 'intimate experiences of drug abuse' or engage in social desirability bias whereby their engagement in the research process is influenced more by who is asking the questions rather than what the questions are. In addition, serious misinterpretations and misapprehensions can be made when outsider-researchers do not understand participant's language, jokes, slang etc. (Windle & Silke, 2019).

I was able to use and understand words distinctive to working class areas of the city, and also ask questions about issues that have not featured in academic publications on the issue of desistance/addiction. In short, not only did this insider knowledge help avoid misunderstands but was a key part of the data collection process and led to the creation of new knowledge. Importantly, it was encouraging for the men to see someone from their community doing research at Ph.D level. For example, P10 reported seeing things in his community that give him the power of example to move on in his life. When I asked him for examples he replied: 'I get it from you'.

All interviews were conducted at the University College Cork campus. In disadvantaged areas of Cork city there are high rates of early school leaving, and few attend university. I left school myself at the age of 13, so know how it feels for someone to think that university is for others—not for people from working class areas. During the first two years of my undergraduate degree I thought someone must have made a mistake by letting me into University! I said to one participant:

> *Graham: "We are in a UCC building at the moment, have you ever thought you would come to a place like this?"*
>
> *P36: "Never did, I came in here today and I thought I would never see my head in the door. People talking about college, I would put up my eyes and say go fuck ye, ye are yuppies".*

I decided at the start of this research project to interview people on the university campus as I wanted to walk people in the gate, to show them that further education was possible, if it was something they wanted. To show them that they too belonged in university. One of great achievements from this project was what happened when one participant asked me how I ended up in college. I explained that I left school at 13 and returned at 29 to start a Level 5 in Adult Continuing Education, and ultimately progressed to doing a Ph.D. This participant explained that he always wanted to go back to education, but having left school early and also being dyslexic, he did not think it possible. I explained to him that I was also dyslexic, and though it can be tough, it can be done: later that day we got a College application form and he applied for a Level 5. He passed that and, at the time of writing, he is planning to start an undergraduate degree. My decision to do my interviews in UCC empowered this man to start his own journey in education.

The literature does, however, warn that insider-research can have negative consequences. As the researcher is sometimes considered to be too close to the culture being studied, insider-research can be accused of bias (Merriam et al., 2001) and lack of critique; although equally, Windle (2021) has shown how a lack of insider knowledge can result in unintentional biases creeping into data collection and analysis. Costerly et al., (2010: 33) warn that insider-researchers must 'also demonstrate' that they 'understand alternative perspectives', although this is surely true of all researchers.

While designing the study, and during the interviews, I remained aware of the possibilities of exhibiting biases, and often reflected on this with my co-authors. This helped me keep an open mind throughout the research and ensured I was aware how to critically evaluate my assumptions regarding participants and the data analysis. To counterbalance potential biases I avoided taking a list of questions into interviews but instead asked each participant one open question:

> *Could you start by telling me what life was like growing up for you?*

With this approach I avoided directing the progress of the interview. Any questions asked after this were led by the participant's life narrative. In addition, I ensured that I clarified any assumptions I had about terminology or shared meanings that might have seemed explicit in the context of the interview, but would not be so obvious to others.

*Of course, grounded theory recognises that we as researchers can never be unbiased or neutral observers. Researchers must ensure, however, that the research reflects the data and, reflects rather than manufactures the phenomenon it describes. Therefore, given the subjectivity that is inherent in all research, and the intensive involvement of the researcher in grounded theory analysis, it was vital that my input be continuously examined, questioned and critiqued (*Charmaz, 2006*).*

Ethics

Ethics permission for this study was granted by the Social Research Ethics Committee (SREC) of University College Cork (UCC). Permission was also granted by each of the gate-holder organisations to engage with their staff with a view to recruiting participants onto the study. UCC and national data protection and data storage regulations were adhered to during this research project. Interviews were transcribed immediately and names were replaced with numbers. In cases where an individual might be identifiable due to place names or experiences, these details were also changed. Consent for participation and publication was sought and re-sought during the interview/research process.

References

Aguiler, J. L. (1981). Insider research: An ethnography of a debate. In D. A. Messerschmidt (Ed.), *Anthropologists at home in North America* (pp. 15–26). Cambridge University Press.

Asselin, M. E. (2003). Insider research: Issues to consider when doing qualitative research in your own setting. *Journal for Nurses in Professional Development, 19*(2), 99–103.

Bell, J. (2005). *Doing your research project*. Open University Press.

Bonner, A., & Tolhurst, G. (2002). Insider-outsider perspectives of participant observation. *Nurse Researcher, 9*(4), 7–19.

Bourgois, P. (1995). *In search of respect: Selling crack in El Barrio*. Cambridge University Press.

Charmaz, K. (2006). *Constructing grounded theory: A practical guide through qualitative analysis*. Sage.

Chavez, C. (2008). Conceptualizing from the inside: Advantages, complications, and demands on insider positionality. *The Qualitative Report, 13*(3), 474–494.

Coghlan, D. (2003). Practitioner research for organizational knowledge: Mechanistic- and organistic-oriented approaches to insider action research. *Management Learning, 34*(4), 451–463.

Costerly, C., Gibbs, P., & Elliott, G. C. (2010). *Doing work based research: Approaches to enquiry for insider-researchers*. Sage.

Farrington, D. (2007). Advancing knowledge about desistance. *Journal of Contemporary Criminal Justice, 23*(1), 125–134.

Healy, D. (2012). *The dynamics of desistance: Charting pathways through change*. Routledge.

Healy, D. (2016). 'I've always tried but I hadn't got the willpower': Understanding pathways to desistance in the Republic of Ireland. In J. Shapland, S. Farrall, & A. Bottoms (Eds.), *Global perspectives on desistance: Reviewing what we know and looking to the future* (pp. 50–65). Routledge.

Healy, D., & O'Donnell, I. (2008). Calling time on crime: Motivation, generativity and agency in Irish probationers. *Probation Journal, 55*(1), 25–38.

Leonard, J., & Windle, J. (2020). 'I could have went down a different path': Talking to people who used drugs problematically and service providers about Irish drug policy alternatives. *International Journal of Drug Policy, 84*, 102891.

Marsh, B. (2011). Narrating desistance: Identity change and the 12-step script. *Irish Probation Journal, 8*(1), 49–68.

Maruna, S. (2001). *Making good: How ex-convicts reform and rebuild their lives*. American Psychological Association Press.

Maruna, S., & Liem, M. (2021). Where is this story going? A critical analysis of the emerging field of narrative criminology. *Annual Review of Criminology, 4*(1), 125–146.

McAdams, D. P. (2001). The psychology of life stories. *Review of General Psychology, 5*(2), 100–122.

Merriam, S. B., Johnson-Bailey, J., Lee, M. Y., Kee, Y., Ntseane, G., & Muhamad, M. (2001). Power and positionality: Negotiating insider/outsider status within and across cultures. *International Journal of Lifelong Education, 20*(5), 405–416.

Mulcahy, J. (2021). Re-storying offending behaviour: A normal response to an overdose of trauma? In O. Lynch, J. Windle, & Y. Amhed (Eds.), *Giving voice to diversity in criminological research: 'Nothing about us without us'* (pp. 89–102). Policy.

Presser, L. (2009). The narratives of offenders. *Theoretical Criminology, 13*(2), 177–200.

Rooney, P. (2005). Researching from the inside—Does it compromise validity? *Level3, 3*(1), 3–19.

Sampson, R., & Laub, J. (1993). Crime and deviance in the life course. *Annual Review of Sociology, 18*(1), 63–84.

Seaman, V., & Lynch, O. (2016). Learning the basics of how to live: Ex-prisoners accounts of doing desistance. *Irish Probation Journal, 16*(1), 65–83.

Shaw, C. (1930). *The Jack-Roller, a delinquent boy's own story*. University of Chicago Press.

Smyth, A., & Holian, R. (2008). Credibility issues in research from within organisations. In P. Sikes & A. Potts (Eds.), *Researching education from the inside* (pp. 41–56). Routledge.

Sutherland, E. (1937). *The professional thief*. University of Chicago Press.

Windle, J. (2021). Reconsidering the 1991 Blackbird Leys Rioters as an underclass: An insider perspective. In O. Lynch, J. Windle, & Y. Ahmed (Eds.), *Giving voice to diversity in criminological research: Nothing about us without us* (pp. 133–148). Policy.

Windle, J., & Silke, A. (2019). Is drawing from the state 'state of the art'? A review of organised crime research data collection and analysis, 2004–2018. *Trends in Organized Crime, 22*(4), 394–413.

CHAPTER 5

Traumatic Childhood and Adolescent Experiences

Abstract Early childhood, child development, interpersonal relationships and the experience of education featured prominently in the analysis of data in this study. Participants reconstructed their experience predominantly using a direct chronological process, recounting early childhood, adolescence then adulthood. The men do this storytelling in a manner that serves to explain how their early experiences were relevant to their later addiction and involvement in crime. The themes of trauma, risk taking, cultural expectations and institutions emerged prominently in the analysis and these themes and related sub-themes are presented here.

Keywords Early childhood experiences · Education · Trauma · Meaning making

This chapter presents the themes that emerged from the grounded theory analysis of the interview data as it relates to early childhood, developmental issues, parenting and education. It provides insight into how participants reconstruct their experience of early childhood including how attribute *motive* to their behaviours in light of their later engagement in crime and problematic alcohol/drug use. Most notably, all participants recalled difficult childhoods and suffered multiple adverse childhood

G. Cambridge et al., *The Desistance Journey*,
https://doi.org/10.1007/978-3-031-11269-0_5

experiences (ACEs) (Dube et al., 2003). Alongside significant traumas in childhood, many identified an ongoing lack of support from teachers at school, experienced bullying whilst in school and reported feeling a sense of shame and stigma attached to the poverty they suffered at home. Many of the participants reflected on being publicly shamed and this was a key memory of their school experience. This experience was often blamed for their lack of educational attainment and ultimately withdrawal from school.

The themes that emerged in this section are presented in chronological order as recalled by the participants. This aligns with what is often found in the use of narrative methods in other criminological research (Maruna, 2001; Presser, 2009) where individuals incorporate their life stories into a narrative that serves the purpose of constructing a coherent tale that gives meaning to their past. In this case, participants' early experiences are portrayed as redemptive suffering and negative childhood experiences are given a purpose in that they *explain* the problem behaviours that emerge later in life. This does not mean that these early experiences are causal in terms of their influence on later behaviour (we cannot know what is causal) but it does mean that these early experiences are an important part of how the participants understand their early years and how they link their issues with addiction and offending with this time period.

This section begins by looking at the challenges and struggles as recalled by the participants while growing up in disadvantaged areas of Cork City; issues of extreme poverty, trauma and neglect were omnipresent in the interview accounts. These accounts dovetail with life histories documented in other recent research conducted in Cork city by Leonard and Windle (2020) and Mulcahy (2021).

Childhood Trauma

The experience of childhood trauma can have serious consequences for a person across their lifespan. Not only are individuals who experience traumatic life experiences over-represented in the criminal justice system, they are also more likely to experience depression, various medical illnesses, as well as a diversity of self-destructive behaviours (Dube et al., 2003; Van der Kolk, 2005). It is important to note that while trauma is known to increase the *risk* of negative outcomes, this is not a foregone conclusion and the impact of trauma depends on things like the level and frequency of trauma experienced (i.e. it is dose-dependent), the existence of social supports and various parental, educational and personal factors, as well as broader socio-economic issues. Not everyone experiences and suffers trauma in the same way. In this study, participants identified a number of significant social problems in their childhood communities, both within the family home and wider area. Poverty, social exclusion, lack of education, trauma and addiction issues dominated participant's recollections of their childhood experiences (also Mulcahy, 2021).

Economic Deprivation

> I dread going home every day. The cupboards would be empty… (P31)

Recollections of poverty dominated the experiences of the men in this study. While participants did not always acknowledge their experience by using the term poverty, most men spoke of a lack of food, warmth, clothes or toys in the home. Most constructed their childhood experiences as negative, marked by neglect, poverty, deprivation, shame and stigma. These experiences were then seamlessly linked to their adult behaviours. Many traced their offending and addiction directly to their experiences of poverty and deprivation. This *narrative* serves the purpose of situating the locus of control for problem behaviours *external* to the individual and also allows for eventual redemption from their past offending. That is, *blame* did not reside in the moral character of the individual, but within the childhood environment (Maruna, 2001). Remember of course that while this analysis focuses on the purpose of the stories individuals tell us and tell themselves, this is to make no judgement on the accuracy, relevance or objectivity of these stories. The telling of the story by the individual serves multiple purposes including to justify their behaviour, to explain their behaviour, to relieve issues of personal guilt regarding any harm caused and to link time periods of their life together in a coherent manner. The issue here is not necessarily to discover an absolute *cause* of addiction or offending—there are many causes and perceived *causes* can change over time and from person to person—but to explore the many complex factors relevant for the individual and others in similar situations.

Many individuals in this study recalled their school experiences also being marred by the shame they felt about poverty and deprivation. Experiencing the stigma of poverty (see Tyler, 2020) and being labelled *poor* by classmates, was a reason that many participants eventually disengaged from education: they wanted to hide their poverty from classmates while simultaneously hoping their situation would be noticed by teachers:

> No lunch, you would be in school starving, hoping someone would give you something. Or the teacher noticed you had nothing and that you get something off the teacher. (P31)

Lack of food had significant consequences for many participants. For example, P31 reported stealing food from others at school, because he was hungry:

> I would have robbed for food at seven [years old]. I would have started taking the lads lunches. In school we would get a bun and a bottle of milk. I would sneak out in the yard and take a few extra buns and eat them, just to have some food. (P31)

The shame was felt more prominently at certain times of the year, for example at back-to-school time and Christmas, as these events shone a spotlight on their poverty and antagonised the stigma that was already there. Many participants spoke of not receiving gifts at Christmas as their parents could not afford toys. P31 and P39 described stealing other children's toys:

> We never got toys, even at Christmas we never got toys. (P31)

> You would be looking at your friends out playing with their toys and you have nothing, your parents were not going to buy them for you, so what are you going to do, go out and nic the thing. (P31)

The men recall how their experience of poverty and deprivation, even in comparison to the other children in their class and community, led them to steal toys and food, both out of necessity and a feeling of exclusion. Participants saw stealing as the only way to access the things other children in their community were given and the men recall feeling a distinct sense of lack of fairness in this situation. This was a theme that reappeared multiple times, the participants routinely pointed to inequality when speaking about how and why they were *forced* to take what they did not have.

Domestic Violence

The majority of participants talked about experiencing traumatic life experiences within the family home, this included physical and emotional abuse and neglect. This treatment often began in early childhood. This finding is not surprising given that we know that individuals with childhood histories of trauma, abuse and neglect account for the majority of people who ultimately end up engaged with the criminal justice system (i.e. Fox et al., 2015; Teplin, et al., 2002).

Witnessing and experiencing violence and cruelty was very common for the men:

> Horse whips, beatings. I was grounded then for weeks up in the room, listening to children outside playing. I would be pulling legs off flies just to pass the day. I used to get fed up and run away again. (P36)

> One time I spilled paint and she stabbed me, it was very violent. (P31)

> My father would punch the head off my mother. (P33)

The violence was just one aspect, but the ongoing hyperarousal and hypervigilance caused by the fear of violence, and the fear of not being safe, was devastating for the men. P19 talked of how the potential for violence within his home meant he always lived in fear:

> There would have been an element of not feeling safe as a child. There were fights in the house; you would say nothing, hid under the bed. ...I never said anything ...never said anything. It was the same in my aunties and uncles house lots of alcohol, shouting fighting breaking the house up, abuse towards us, it was very hard growing up in that environment. (P19)

The men linked the experience of violence to their own self of self-worth and self-esteem. They reflected on how the violence impacted their confidence and their ability to form relationships but also how, via the mechanism of social learning, witnessing adult violence influenced their own behaviour as adults (see Freyd et al., 2005). They reported how, as adults, they themselves had become violent (see Dong et al., 2004), and how they very quickly saw the role of drugs and alcohol in soothing the emotions underpinning these behaviours and the associated memories of violence, abuse and neglect (see Cicchetti & Toth, 1995; Leonard & Windle, 2020; Maté, 2012; Van der Kolk, 2005):

> I did not know how to cope with it [violence at home], and the first time I drank, I sniffed a bag of glue the same night, and I went back for it, then everything went out the window, school and everything. (P10)

Addiction and Parental Neglect

Van der Kolk (2005, p. 2) highlights the importance of secure childhoods, whereby children are supported and cared for, and that these are rare amongst 'children exposed to alcoholic parents or domestic violence' (also Troy & Sroufe, 1987). Several participants referred to their own parent's struggles with addiction and the heavy drinking and drug taking witnessed in the family home in the generations before them. As a result, despite their awareness of the negative consequences, alcohol and drug abuse were normalised and even glorified.

> But the drugs.... I saw in my mother's house drugs were acceptable, because they were all enjoying themselves, taking Es partying. It looked fun. (P19)

The men recalled how the fun was short-lived, and partying led to the neglect of the children. The neglect was related to the basic needs of food, warmth and access to education, but also to psychological needs including discipline, structure, positive role models and attention. P27 felt that his parents were not physically or emotionally supportive due to their own addictions:

> I grow up in an alcoholic home, the parents were heavy drinkers, there was no one ever checking on me, it was a dysfunctional home. (P27)

The men also spoke about how this neglect led to opportunity. A lack of supervision meant that the boys were free to do whatever they wished with few consequences:

> There was no one looking after us, we were breaking windows, taking chases, I can remember there was no park in the area, we were just running around gallivanting. (P20)

> There was no discipline back then, in my life there was not anyway. The truth be told my old man did not give a fuck what I done. He was out … drinking 24 seven, fighting, that was his life, he grow up that way. (P13)

School

Overwhelmingly, education was not prioritised by the men's parents. As a result, the men themselves did not see school as something that would benefit them, at least when they were young. Most adults they knew had left school early and gained employment in manual labour or were unemployed. Education was not a priority, nor was it associated with better employment prospects; commonly participants rebelled and got into trouble at school (see Leonard, 2021; Willis, 1977). Furthermore, not only was it difficult for the men to study when they were hungry and tired, many reported that the poverty of the family home resulted in them being the target of bullying in school. The men point out that they were stigmatised by both peers and teachers, and they internalised this shame. This presented yet another barrier to learning. Feelings of disenfranchisement and actual exclusion from school led to the emergence of aggressive and disruptive behaviours and some of the participants were eventually permanently expelled.

> At the end of first year I was gone, Can't remember why, I was kicked out. (P14)

In addition to the structural limits and boundaries placed upon their education, the participants spoke of the irrelevance of education given their own personal circumstances. Being hungry, tired and neglected meant their priorities lay elsewhere. Some viewed school as a barrier to full-time employment, and assumed that their life trajectory was predetermined to exclude further education. Mostly the men thought that education was for other people. Many spoke of their ignorance of any relationship between education and employment and, the potential for education to provide their choice and mobility in the job market:

> I remember thinking in school, when I am 18 I will just go and get a job. I thought that was the way life was. (P24)

> I started to go working in a factory at 14. I told them I was 16. (P18)

> I never saw education as way of making a few quid. (P31)

In addition to the assumptions the men had about school, they spoke of interpersonal issues they had with teachers and other students. Many recalled being treated badly and suffering the stigmatisation. P13 recollects of being mocked for wearing a dirty uniform.

> No, I did not want to be there, you would be going to school with a manky [dirty] uniform, you are getting the piss taken out of you left right and centre, by teachers and pupils. (P13)

Participants associated their aggressive or disruptive behaviours directly with this sense of shame and linked it to the bullying they experienced at the hands of both teachers and pupils. They felt excluded, and reported a strong sense of not belonging, of not fitting in.

> So then you are going in there telling them [teachers] to fuck off, telling them to mind their own business, fuck you I do not want to be here, then you were put up against the wall for the day, that's not school, teachers did not give a fuck about you back then. (P13)

Adolescence and Teenage Years: Being Bored, Taking Risks and Rites of Passage

In addition to stealing food and toys that their parents could not afford, participants reported engaging in transgressive crime, i.e. crime that causes harm but is perhaps less serious from a legal perspective, for example, graffiti and destruction of property versus assault. Criminologists, such as Katz (1988), have long identified the thrill of crime as an antidote to boredom and a means to escape the monotony of life. A *thrilling undertaking* that was common amongst many participants was joyriding: stealing cars/motorbikes and driving them at high speeds, usually ending in crashing or at least severely damaging the vehicle. Joyriding became popular in Cork's Northside working-class communities during the 1980s and 1990s, as it did in many working-class communities across Ireland (McCullough et al., 1990) and also the UK (Windle, 2021). Many participants started joyriding at a young age: P31 stole his first motorbike when he was just 11 years old.

McVerry (2003) highlighted the shared background of young people who engaged in joyriding across Ireland as individuals from 'deprived housing estates, with inadequate facilities and services' and engage in high-risk activities that confer no material gain save the thrill of the risk itself. Commentators have linked joyriding to the experience of economic deprivation and social exclusion, and represent it as a means of relieving the boredom and mundanity of everyday life (Griffin & Kelleher, 2010; also Campbell, 1993; Windle, 2021): they 'live for the present because they see no future… [they] feel that they, and their communities, have been abandoned' (McVerry, 2003, p. 86). For Campbell (1993, p. 41) joyriders are motivated by a 'commitment to pure pleasure, pride in the performance' and an opportunity to prove their masculinity. In this sense, and as will be discussed in later chapters, their addiction issues oftentimes emerged initially as a continuation of this youthful thrill-seeking. Indeed, some spoke of the thrill of 'getting into trouble' and joyriding. For them, risk-taking behaviour led to a sense of control and of self-realisation where normally they felt powerless in their everyday lives:

> I thrived on that, I could not walk out the door without trouble, I had to have it. (P21)

Apart from the excitement, and sense of power, associated with joyriding, participants identified how stealing cars was common in their community and amongst their peer group. It was seen as normal:

> I bumped into a few fellows, they all had screw drivers. They were going robbing cars, it was a normal thing to do on a Wednesday night [in the estate]. (P15)

Furthermore, older joyriders often became local celebrities (see Campbell, 1993) and ultimately role models.

> Oh yah, sure they were *the shit* like. When they joyride on Kilmore Road...it was like something you would see on TV....... They [joyriders] were really looked up to. (P20)

Participants described a process of engaging in increasingly more serious risk-taking behaviour which they linked to negative early childhood experiences. In the case of joyriding, participants described choosing to steal and destroy cars because they lacked access to money and leisure resources, did not or could not engage in education and lacked any adult supervision:

> You would get bored, so you rob cars and bikes…You could be robbing horses or anything. (P6)

Participants also pointed to parental neglect, and lack of supervision, as providing an opportunity to transgress, but also that the lack of supervision meant that there were few if any pro-social role models for young people to meaningfully engage with in their community:

> We never had nothing or no-one or a chance at life and stuff, growing up in the 90s in [Northside estate] was hard. We had [the] youth club all right, but they would only leave certain people in. (P20)

They described their early psychological disengagement from school, followed by physical disengagement as they left or were excluded. This ultimately left them hanging around the streets with like-minded peers. There are parallels in the experiences of the men with the main findings of Hirschi's (1969) social control theory: he states that a failure to form and maintain positive social bonds with mainstream society can lead to disenfranchisement and ultimately criminal or deviant behaviour. In this theory, the family environment is the foundation of attachment, in the first instance parents act as role models and teach their children acceptable behaviours. This was not the case for the men interviewed for this book. Indeed, P20's assessment of his own parents as role models is instructive:

> My mam did not work, my father was a drug dealer. (P20)

All participants recognised the role of poverty, social exclusion and lack of opportunity as formative in their teenage years and highlighted how risk-taking behaviour became a means of escaping the social limitations placed on them, but also as a means of solidifying an identity for themselves. Multiple ethnographic studies conducted in Ireland and the UK and US (see Anderson, 1999; Bourgois, 1995; Hourigan, 2011; Windle, 2019, 2021; Winlow, 2001), have highlighted how working-class men respond to economic and social exclusion by searching for alternative ways of 'doing' masculinity (Messerschmidt, 1993; also Carlsson, 2013). They can do this by using drugs, engaging in crime and other transgressions to demonstrate that they are tough, smart, autonomous and fearless. For the men in this study their early thrill-seeking behaviours represented the beginning of developing their tough man identity. This identity became influential in their slide into addiction and ultimately served as a barrier to their recovery.

Role Models and Learning to be a 'Hard Man'

Another theme that emerged quite strongly in the analysis of the interviews was that of peer influence and the importance of role models. For the participants, when they were young, the individuals they looked up to were heavy consumers of alcohol and drugs, and routinely engaged in crime and violence; these were the activities which made them desirable role models, and this tough lifestyle was so valued by and attractive to participants they imitated it from an early-age. Participants described prioritising the risk-taking behaviours they witnessed amongst their peers and attempting to mirror these behaviours to ensure acceptance within the community but also to consolidate their own 'hard-man' image.

While we refer to street culture in this book, we are not suggesting that there is only one community or one culture within Cork's Northside; there are various and multiple overlapping communities, each with its own subculture/s. What is relevant here is that the men in this study, and many other men who come from communities marked by economic deprivation, tend to prioritise a particular subculture that revolves around hegemonic masculinity.

However it is important to note that peer imitation is normal and expected amongst all adolescents, not just those who engage in criminal activity. Seeking to push, oppose, or rebel against, social norms is a normal developmental teenage stage. Nonetheless, decades of research have shown that peer group interactions are influential in identity creation and learned behaviour, including behaviour which can be harmful (Allen et al., 2003; for example, Sutherland, 1949). That is, young people can learn both positive and negative values and norms from peers, both of which can become internalised.

For participants in this study, their isolation from mainstream or pro-social peer relationships, their neglect by parents and near total lack of adult supervision enhanced the influence of problematic peer groups and accelerated the adoption of anti-social norms and, an identity based on often oppositional and defiant behaviours. However, the men also recall the negative influence of parental relationships, beyond the neglect they recall:

> I was never even shown how to shave by my old fella. So my perception of what it was to be a man changed throughout the years. (P24)

> He was my idol growing up. He was a womanizer a heavy alcoholer, just tough man...I made him a bigger person than he really was as a young fella. He was someone I aspired to be. (P30)

> The people I looked up to were the people on the street corners, people who could fight. (P37)

Apart from the normal developmental processes and the influence of peers on self and social identity, the dynamics between younger and older people in a particular community can also be influential. The RAPID areas of Cork City suffered decades of transgenerational poverty, unemployment, substance abuse and criminality, consequently, the density of role models who routinely engaged in heavy drug taking and drinking, violence, crime (especially drug dealing), and who had been in prison, increased the likelihood that the social norms associated with these behaviours were prominent amongst young people growing up in the area:

> my role models were the fellas getting out of jail, They would have money from drug dealing. (P31)

> They had the nice clothes, they had nice cars, the jewellery, there were no other role models there... it was inevitable to go like that. (P19)

> It's not like other parts of the city where it is encouraged to go to college, or the next- door neighbour was a doctor, it was just joyriding, drug dealing, that was just the thing, people were going to prison it was desirable among young people, it was like a badge of honour, or it was something you just done as a teenager. (P15)

The lads our participants looked up to were spending the money they made from acquisitive crime and drug dealing on drugs and alcohol. They were well-liked, partly because they spent their money on others, which provided them with a positive ***hard man*** identity and gave them a powerful status within their community.

> Every weekend he would be after doing a stroke, (robbery) and we see him on a Sunday and he would be after getting a couple of grand, bring everyone on for the day. (P24)

Imitating these older youths and men helped participants see themselves as one of the lads, it was a way of making themselves fit in as part of the group. Participants understandably prioritised this in-group identity and actively sought inclusion through imitation. Similar processes are well documented elsewhere (i.e. Anderson, 1999) and mirror what Tomsen (2008) describes as 'protest masculinity': a gender identity that is characteristic of men seeking a masculine claim on power due to other options being denied by economic and social exclusion.

Participants discussed getting involved in criminal activity in order to make a name for themselves within their community, and specifically within their peer group. Their older peers, however, often took advantage of the younger generation's eagerness to be seen as a hard man, for example some participants reported storing or holding drugs for older peers. While this is of course exploitation of a vulnerable youth, the kids themselves saw this involvement as providing them credibility, belonging and purpose (see Windle et al., 2020):

> They used to do it to everyone. If you went down there today it would still be happened, kids running around with a handfull of Es. (P34)

Once involved in criminal activity, participants learned by following older peers who exploited their eagerness to be part of the group (see Windle et al., 2020). In addition to the desire to belong, the outcome of engaging with anti-social peers is the ongoing social learning impact; Sutherland (1949) suggested that much criminal behaviour is learned through association with other people. These connections provide a forum for acquiring techniques as well as motives, drives, rationalisations and attitudes. This differential association provides people with the knowledge, skills and identity that encourages them to interpret situations as potential opportunities for offending:

> There was a good group of us, about 12, two different age groups, there would have been the younger crowd, and they would be watching what we were doing and they were following suit. (P13)

Early Employment

One individual who took part in this study mentioned that he started working at a young age, however, his employment was made precarious by a combination of his heavy drinking and the economic downturn. He was the exception, however, as most participants had never been employed, or had experienced only very sporadic employment.

> No, I never worked a day in my life... I know now today it was me and addiction, addiction was the reason. (P36)

> Have you work previously? (Graham)

> Nothing worth talking about. (P34)

> Was there every any jobs, opportunity's ambitions? (Graham)

> No, there was none. (P34)

With minimal or no education or work history, many participants spent a lot of their time on the streets. Here they learnt a necessary street culture that emphasised masculinity, prioritised avoiding being seen as weak or a fool and challenged any and all authority; taking orders was seen as a sign of weakness. In addition, as seen in other studies, not working was often viewed as evidence of hegemonic masculinity which was highly valued within the street culture (see Anderson, 1999):

> People ask me was I working, my attitude was *I am in my bollocks*, I work for nobody, that was my attitude…I would not work for other people, they must think I am an eejit.

However, as the men got older some reflected on the role that employment played in helping with recovery and desistance. Those who did work recognised that the structure provided by employment ensured that the chaos of their lives on the streets was kept in check, if even for a short while.

It kept me off the streets it kept me some bit sane away from the madness. (P18)

Conclusion

This short account of the early experiences of the participants in this study provides a snapshot of some of the poverty, neglect, abuse and trauma experienced by young people in deprived areas of Cork City. Participants recall witnessing violence and substance abuse in their homes, they recounted developing a disdain for education, they reflected on the stigma attached to poverty and spoke of the role their family had in explicitly and implicitly encouraging risky behaviours. There were few positive role models—no 'one good adult'—and significant intergenerational transmission of trauma, alcohol/drug abuse and criminal behaviour. These boys had very little working in their favour, they suffered tough lives, and were at high risk of engaging in addiction and crime.

These narratives correspond to the findings from several strands of academic research. A key finding that repeatedly emerges in situations such as those described by the men in this study is the emergence of subcultural adaptions as a response to economic disadvantage and social exclusion. Not only do some residents of impoverished areas develop informal rules to guide behaviour, these rules also influence local people's identities and behaviours. Such 'codes' often centre upon using violence and risky behaviour to develop a valued masculine status (Anderson, 1999; in Ireland, Hourigan, 2011; Windle, 2019). For many living in these areas, legitimate opportunities for both work and leisure are limited, but illegitimate opportunities for making money, gaining status and leisure are plentiful.

Anderson (1999) notes that the rules governing these local subcultures are influenced by economic deprivation and social marginalisation, but are also transgenerational: they are passed down from parent to children, who are then socialised by their peers. This conforms to another finding prominent in the participant's narratives— the impact of their parenting experience, or lack of it, on their behaviour.

A growing body of academic research has identified the long-term impacts associated with experiencing cumulative adverse childhood experiences (ACEs) (see Lambert & Gill-Emerson, 2017). There are nine broad traditional ACEs: verbal abuse, substance abuse in the family, physical abuse, emotional neglect, mental illness in the family, loss of a parent, domestic violence, sexual abuse, incarcerated family members and physical neglect. More recent studies have, however, begun to connect family and individual experiences with community adversity. Ellis and Dietz (2017) have argued, in terms of ACEs, structural issues (i.e. poverty, discrimination, lack of social capital) represent the 'soil' out of which individual experiences grow and develop.

While many of the population experience some of the nine traditional ACEs as a child, the culmination of multiple ACEs is a risk factor for various physical and mental health issues across the life course. For example, Dube and colleagues (2003, p. 389) found that people with more than five ACEs were 'seven–tenfold more likely to report illicit drug use problems, addiction to illicit drugs, and parenteral drug use'. Ford and colleagues (2020) found that just under half (46 percent) of individuals imprisoned in a Welsh prison had suffered four or more ACEs.

All of the men in this study reported experiencing multiple ACEs, and all had suffered significant trauma as children and young people. Experiencing trauma does not, however, mean that you will commit a crime or become addicted to alcohol or drugs. Equally, growing up in an economically deprived area does not mean you will experience multiple ACEs or commit crime or become addicted to alcohol or drugs. But localised economic deprivation and social exclusion, coupled with exclusion from education, neglect, abuse and the opportunity to engage in risk-taking behaviour make things very difficult for young people in all aspects of their lives.

References

Allen, M., Donohue, W. A., Griffin, A., Ryan, D., & Turner, M. (2003). Comparing the influence of parents and peers on the choice to use drugs: A meta-analytic summary of the literature. *Criminal Justice and Behavior, 30*(2), 163–186.

Anderson, E. (1999). *Code of the street: Decency, violence, and the moral life of the inner city*. Norton.

Bourgois, P. (1995). *In search of respect: Selling crack in El Barrio*. Cambridge University Press.

Campbell, B. (1993). *Goliath: Britain's dangerous places*. Methuen.

Carlsson, C. (2013). Masculinities, persistence and desistence. *Criminology, 51*(3), 661–693.

Cicchetti, D., & Toth, S. L. (1995). Developmental psychopathology and disorders of affect. In D. Cicchetti & D. J. Cohen (Eds.), *Developmental psychopathology* (pp. 369–420). John Wiley.

Dong, M., Anda, R. F., Felitti, V. J., Dube, S. R., Williamson, D. F., Thompson, T. J., Loo, C. M., & Giles, W. H. (2004). The interrelatedness of multiple forms of childhood abuse, neglect, and household dysfunction. *Child Abuse and Neglect, 28*(7), 771–784.

Dube, S. R., Felitti, V. J., Dong, M., Chapman, D. P., Giles, W. H., & Anda, R. F. (2003). Childhood abuse, neglect, and household dysfunction and the risk of illicit drug use: The adverse childhood experiences study. *Pediatrics, 111*(3), 564–572.

Ellis, W. R., & Dietz, W. H. (2017, September–October). A new framework for addressing adverse childhood and community experiences: The building community resilience model. *Academic Pediatrics, 17*(7S), S86–S93. https://doi.org/10.1016/j.acap.2016.12.011. PMID: 28865665.

Ford, K., Bellis, M. A., Hughes, K., Barton, E. R., & Newbury, A. (2020). Adverse childhood experiences: A retrospective study to understand their associations with lifetime mental health diagnosis, self-harm or suicide attempt, and current low mental wellbeing in a male Welsh prison population. *Health and Justice, 8*(1), 1–13.

Fox, B. H., Perez, N., Cass, E., Baglivio, M. T., & Epps, N. (2015). Trauma changes everything: Examining the relationship between adverse childhood experiences and serious, violent and chronic juvenile offenders. *Child Abuse and Neglect, 46*(2), 163–173.

Freyd, J., Klest, B., & Allard, C. (2005). Betrayal trauma: Relationship to physical health, psychological distress, and a written disclosure intervention. *Journal of Trauma and Dissociation, 6*(3), 83–104.

Griffin, M., & Kelleher, P. (2010). Uncertain futures: Men on the margins in Limerick City. *Irish Probation Journal, 7*(1), 24–46.

Hirschi, T. (1969). *Causes of delinquency*. University of California Press.

Hourigan, N. (2011). *Understanding limerick*. Cork University Press.

Katz, J. (1988). *Seductions of crime*. Basic Books.

Lambert, S., & Gill-Emerson, G. (2017). *ACEs at Cork Simon: Exploring the connection between early trauma and later negative life events among Cork Simon service users*. Simon Community.

Leonard, J. (2021). An autobiographical account of desistance and recovery. In O. Lynch, J. Windle & Y. Ahmed (Eds.), *Giving voice to diversity in criminological research: Nothing about us without us* (pp.149–156). Policy.

Leonard, J., & Windle, J. (2020). I could have went down a different path: Talking to people who used drugs problematically and service providers about Irish drug policy alternatives. *International Journal of Drug Policy*.

Maruna, S. (2001). *Making good: How ex-convicts reform and rebuild their lives.* American Psychological Association Press.
Maté, G. (2012). Addiction: Childhood trauma, stress and the biology of addiction. *Journal of Restorative Medicine, 1*(1), 56–63.
McCullough, D., Schmidt, T., & Lockhart, B. (1990). *Car theft in Northern Ireland: Recent studies on a persistent problem.* Extern.
McVerry, P. (2003). *Joyriders: The meaning is in the shadows.* Veritas.
Messerschmidt, J. (1993). *Masculinities and crime.* Rowman and Littlefield.
Mulcahy, J. (2021). Re-storying offending behaviour: A normal response to an overdose of trauma? In O. Lynch, J. Windle, & Y. Amhed (Eds.), *Giving voice to diversity in criminological research: 'Nothing about us without us'* (pp. 89-102). Policy.
Presser, L. (2009). The narratives of offenders. *Theoretical Criminology, 13*(2), 177–200.
Sutherland, E. H. (1949). *Principles of criminology.* Lippinccot.
Teplin, L. A., Abram, K. M., McClelland, G. M., Dulcan, M. K., & Mericle, A. A. (2002). Psychiatric disorders in youth in juvenile detention. *Archives of General Psychiatry, 59*(12), 1133–1143.
Tomsen, S. (2008). Masculinities, crime, and criminalisation. In T. Anthony & C. Cunneen (Eds.), *Theoretical criminology companion* (pp. 94–104). Hawkins Press.
Troy, M., & Sroufe, L. (1987). Victimization among preschoolers: Role of attachment relationship history. *Journal of the American Academy of Child and Adolescent Psychiatry, 26*(2), 166–172.
Tyler, I. (2020). *Stigma: The machinery of inequality.* Bloomsbury.
Van der Kolk, B. (2005). Developmental trauma disorder: Towards a rational diagnosis for children with complex trauma histories. *Psychiatric Annals, 35*(5), 401–408.
Van der Kolk, B. (2014). *The body keeps the score.* Penguin.
Willis, P. (1977). *Learning to labour: How working class kids get working class jobs.* Routledge.
Windle, J. (2019). The causes and consequences of gangland violence in the Republic of Ireland. In R. Lombardo (Ed.), *Organized crime: Causes and consequences* (pp.110–123). Nova Science.
Windle, J. (2021). Reconsidering the 1991 Blackbird Leys Rioters as an underclass: an insider perspective. In O. Lynch, J. Windle, & Y. Ahmed (Eds.), *Giving voice to diversity in criminological research: Nothing about us without us* (pp. 133–148). Policy.
Windle, J., Moyle, L., & Coomber, R. (2020). 'Vulnerable' kids going country: Children and young people's involvement in county lines drug dealing. *Youth Justice, 20*(1–2), 64–78.
Winlow, S. (2001). *Badfellas crime, tradition and new masculinities.* Berg.

CHAPTER 6

Lifestyle, Offending, and Addiction

Abstract This chapter presents some of the themes that emerged from this study of men from the Cork area who experienced addiction and involvement in criminal activity. This chapter recalls the themes that emerged from the analysis of stories the men tell of their journey into crime and addiction as teenagers and young adults. The stories are replete with accounts of the influence of peers, issues of vulnerability, victimisation, peer pressure, cultural expectations and the lack of viable life alternatives; issues of social identity dominate. The issue of performative masculinity was also a central emergent theme as was a sense of impending and actual loss of control. The loss of control was across all life domains. The chapter culminates with the accounts of the men who ultimately experienced prison, and how this influenced their journey(ies) into desistance and recovery.

Keywords Narrative · Loss of control · Prison · Recovery

This chapter explores the participants' accounts of their lifestyle, including offending, whilst in active addiction. Participant narratives often centred on their community and how it was dominated by violence, crime and addiction and, the interaction between their early personal experience and this community context. Many identified their behaviour as

G. Cambridge et al., *The Desistance Journey*,
https://doi.org/10.1007/978-3-031-11269-0_6

being a response to their environment whereby being violent and tough served a protective function. This chapter tracks the development of the men out of their traumatic childhoods and adolescence described in the last chapter. As the participants recall this stage of their lives, many reflected on their behaviours as self-harming and understood their addictive behaviours as a form of self-medication aimed at soothing the pain of early childhood experiences. This framing of their drug use is a part of their recovery/desistance narrative and serves many functions for the men, primarily allowing them to account for their choice to engage in substance abuse, their *lack of personal control* or an *inevitability* around their addiction and a means of linking their traumatic childhood to their adult selves. Again the issue here is not whether the framing is *true* or not, but how the men tell their story to make meaning of their past, for both themselves and others.

Imitation or social learning is another theme which follows on from the previous chapter—that is, participants learned behaviour from peer groups and family members. From the outside, some behaviour may appear as destructive and harmful but, for many participants, it was a means of self-protection and survival. What would ultimately become destructive initially served a specific function; that function may have been using drugs to sooth pain or using violence to build a reputation which would deter victimisation. Learned behaviours had developmental but also strategic elements. Indeed, some spoke of crime and substance use as therapeutic: they were a means of escaping from trauma, hurt, boredom and helplessness. While excess drinking and drug taking were initially seen as having strategic and/or therapeutic benefits, those behaviours quickly became problematic as addiction overtook choice, and generated even more harm and trauma. Regardless of the initial motive for engaging in crime and substance use, all participants ended up on the same road: one leading to mental ill health, suicide attempts, overdoses and prison.

Social Identity: Self-Preservation and Masculinity

Manifestations of masculinity dominated the accounts of all participants. While this was not always explicitly described as such by the men, it was a key organising feature for the men's behaviour and also a justification for their actions. The performative element of masculinity, of doing masculinity (Messerschmidt, 1993; see Carlsson, 2012), was central to all accounts. The men recalled the importance of being seen to behave in ways which highlighted the form of masculinity they felt was acceptable within their community: behaviours which participants describe as part of being a man, particularly behaviours associated with being a hard man.

The identity itself was fundamentally linked with the values prioritised by their community. The hard-man reputation was not necessarily about the self and one's sense of self—but about power over others and status in the group. The hard-man culture can be compared with the street code witnessed by Anderson (1999) in the US and road culture witnessed by Gunter (2017) in the UK, and discovered in Sweden by Carlsson (2012). In some respects it may be an exaggerated version of what Connell (2005; Connell & Messerschmidt, 2005) calls hegemonic masculinity. This is not merely a form of masculinity identified amongst offenders and violent communities but, to some degree, the dominant style of masculinity performed in many Western societies. This type of masculinity is about displays of power and dominance, and reinforcing traditional gender roles where men dominate women and other men often using violence, or threatened violence. It is a means of gaining social approval and, achieving status and power, and for some communities it is the only means of social mobility. Achieving status in the community involves engaging in performative masculinity in order to gain visibility and respect, albeit feared respect. When people are denied recourse to other forms of status—notably through employment and education—hegemonic masculinity, or being a hard-man, may be the only means through which some can achieve status and power within their community (see also Willis, 1977). This performance of masculinity always comes at the expense of others and ultimately the individual themselves.

The men in this research had little or no education and, at best, a chequered employment history. This eroded their self-esteem and confidence and other sources of self-esteem were channelled in the absence of experiences traditionally linked to positive self-worth. Status and self-respect were sought through violence, crime and consumption. The men in this research describe how they focused on external social rewards, hoping this would improve their sense of self. They talked about using violence and intimidation as the only means through which they felt able to gain confidence (see Messerschmidt, 1993) while creating a reputation as a hard man.

What many would consider negative experiences, such as getting stabbed or being imprisoned, became important symbols of masculinity for many participants. These events even afforded them celebrity status within their community:

> You were [seen as] tougher because you were stabbed. (P15)

> They would look up to you, when you get out first [of prison], you'd have celebrity status. (P27)

Such recognition gave the men a sense of achievement and power within their community (see Willis, 1977). Many participants identified violence as being valued within their community, and the only available means of gathering respect:

> You were respected if you fought, you were not respected if you could debate, you were not respected because you were intelligent, you were respected if you were not afraid to fight. You did not need to be a good fighter, once you were willing to go into a fight in the first place. (P15)

Many of the men still hark after this respect today, even though they now recognise the dangers that such an approach presents to their well-being:

> Amazing, fucking hell, I would still have traits of that today, and that can kind of kick in now and again, the ego, but at the end it was fuck, respect like, people respected me. (P20)

While there were ***highs*** associated with the power and violence, ultimately the masculine identities they projected to others in their social group and community were considered a vital means of survival—they identified their behaviour as a form of self-protection. The ***hard-man*** reputation depended upon creating, and then maintaining, a credible threat of violence (see Anderson, 1999), and without this, they would be subject to the violence they threatened on others. Ultimately, this behaviour promoted power and a means of control in dangerous and chaotic environments:

> I felt the bravado, and I thought it was a great thing and I thought that people would have been looking at me differently. (P9)

> To have power over people, to have people afraid of you, to have them do anything for you that was my idea as power. (P26)

Some were not violent but felt the need to give the impression that they could 'handle themselves' in a manner similar to what Goffman (1967) described as keeping-face. Being physically capable of violence, and being willing to use it, was seen as the foundational characteristics for being a man. These characteristics were the antithesis of being weak, and being seen as weak increased the chance of victimisation (see Anderson, 1999):

> I never saw myself as a handy or a hard-man, but I tried to lead-on that I could, I tried to give off that impression, so you would not be seen as weak. (P15)

Weakness was described as both a personality trait and physical state. To be seen as weak was problematic because you were low in the street hierarchy and that meant you were vulnerable. Participants felt that those seen as weak would be taken advantage of. Indeed, research by Anderson (1999) and Mullins (2006) supports this notion of a hierarchy within street culture, whereby those who do not gain respect from their peers are dominated and exploited by those with higher status (also Windle & Briggs, 2015; Windle et al., 2020).

For the men, strategies to avoid being seen as weak were simple: prove to others that you're tough and can handle yourself when needed. This inevitably involved *performative* displays of violence and avoiding behaviour that could be seen as weak. This is known as ***doing masculinity***, performing in a certain way in order to project a particular identity. One participant, for example, described avoiding crying in public:

> I would be embarrassed over crying and stuff like that. (P8)

Another element of this identity was a particular loyalty to the community. The ***rules*** of the street often preclude sharing information outside the group, especially avoiding being labelled 'a rat'; that is, cooperating with the Gardaí (police). Not only did some identify cooperating with the Gardaí as a sign of weakness, but being labelled 'a rat' would very likely result in being ostracized from the community and increase the chance of victimisation:

> I would have rather went in [prison] and done my time .... because I would have wanted the name that I was ok rather than a rat. (P18)

> You would lose your place in society [for collaborating with the Gardaí]; people would treat me like shit again. (P31)

While there was an element of protection to be gained from adhering to the street rules, maintaining a hard-man identity had its disadvantages: notably, others would want to fight you in an effort to demonstrate their own masculinity. Indeed, participants identified how they had sought to fight those individuals with a reputation for violence as a means of increasing their own status, and others had done the same to them when they had gained a sufficient reputation.

> I had a name and a reputation, so fellas were fighting with me for their reputations, at this stage it was all reputation. I was doing the macho thing again. (P21)

For the men in this study, masculinity was a zero-sum game—being tough was a commodity that could be taken by other people or retained at the expense of other people. This dynamic meant that there was a constant struggle to seek or maintain the image.

P21's drive to maintain his hard-man image resulted in him resorting to violence, even when he did not want to fight, and when it was obvious violence was causing him harm. His family home was attacked in a shooting and he felt that failure to retaliate would diminish his hard-won reputation (Mullins, 2006). He was torn between the need to maintain face on the streets and avoid trouble at home and with the police. The quote below echoes Goffman's (1967) observation regarding the front and backstage personas:

> I would be crying upstairs, tough man down-stairs, upstairs I was crying knowing what I was doing was wrong. I could not separate myself, [my] reputation was more important. I could not go out the door, I would have all the intentions to say '*boys I can't do it*', but once I got out that door I could not walk away from it. (P21)

Vulnerability: Fear, Respect and Self-Preservation

Being violent, avoiding violence and thinking about violence were a routine part of participants' daily lives. For example, the threat of violence dictated where they travelled and who they travelled with. Ending up in the wrong area of the city could have disastrous consequences. Not only was the preoccupation with developing a hard-man reputation important for status, but it was also directly linked to survival within their community (see Anderson, 1999). Participants felt that to be respected they needed to be seen to be capable of 'looking after themselves', i.e. able and willing to use violence successfully. They repeatedly told the interviewer that if they did not show others that they were willing to defend themselves, they would be seen as weak and so targeted by others in their community.

This required being willing to *stand up for yourself* regardless of who the opponent was. Showing fear was a sign of weakness. The act of *standing up for yourself* was enough to gather respect—you did not have to win the fight, but you did have to give it a go:

> Respect, we got respect and we were left alone, that was the key - we were left alone. For us then we could walk through Mayfield and the hard fellas were up in the corner [and] a lot of [other] people [had to] go around the long way......we could go straight on because [of] what we done and we were fearless, even though they would test us, by calling us a langer, a prick. You would have to stand up to them. And many a time I would have got a clatter, a beating, but I stood up again and got more respect for it. (P39)

Being publicly disrespected could not be tolerated and retaliation was expected (see Anderson, 1999). Indeed, backing down and failing to retaliate could be risky—it was seen to signal weakness and, consequently, to increase the risk of victimisation. Surviving within the community required participants to always show a willingness to use violence.

The men learned these lessons at a very young age, and their accounts make clear that early childhood traumas were not just an outcome of family life but their community environment:

> When I was a kid and my mam would send me to the shop, I would get robbed 8 times out of 10. So I started fighting from a young age. (P34)

> I learned how to adjust quick, how this place operates, how you have to be, how to stand up for yourself, that was my mentality growing up. If people in the area seen you as weak target they would intimidate you, for me, I had to make a name and quick. (P37)

For some, there was a clear disjuncture between home and street lives. Some participant's parents disagreed with violence, yet knew their children had to learn how to handle themselves:

> My mother and father were lovely people, they raised us right...but [I knew] that if I pulled away from it [the hard-man identity], they would turn on me because I would have *got soft*. It was all bravado, who is hard, fuck the guards, fuck the law, fuck authority, there will be no one tell us anything. (P39)

Other parents, however, recognised the reality of the area and actively prepared their children for the inevitable violence they were going to encounter:

> At home we always were into boxing, my dad is still interested in boxing, he would have boxed when he was younger, even on the streets, there was that mentality that you have to be tough, if someone hit you, you would have to hit them back. (P16)

> He would have told me to stand up for myself in school, if you got into a fight even at a young age they would ask you who won the fight. (P16)

Regardless of the home environment, as youths and adults, their behaviour was socially reinforced by peers on the streets. Quite simply, being violent meant that others treated them better:

> If I went out and shot someone, or done something tomorrow, they would be back there treating me nicer. (P34)

Feuding

For the men in this study, violence served multiple functions in addition to gaining respect. But the role of and the importance of violence in the community meant that minor incidents could spiral and had the potential to escalate into serious feuds. Feuds were often linked to local history and, group, family and community identities. Given the importance of social identity for the participants, they describe how the imperative to respond to violence with violence was almost obligatory, that it was not just about the individual, but about the family/community. The feud was often linked to family pride, and entire generations of individuals in a family felt they would be ridiculed and disrespected for not responding (see Hourigan et al., 2018; Katz, 1988; Marsh, 2019; Windle, 2019):

> They were getting more and more violent; I started fighting with a lot of people I grew up with. They actually turned into feuds to be honest, weapons being used and everything; I was stabbed when I was 17. (P8)

> You Would be ridiculed, by the family. (P20)

There was and still is a lot of routine violence on the Northside of Cork City between groups of young lads. While this is often the outcome of arguments between intoxicated groups of young people, the fighting could easily escalate to draw in the wider community. Oftentimes, family and friends would retaliate to secure the group or family reputation and this had a contagion-like effect:

> I seen the man I was fighting pull out a screw driver, so I covered my face and he got me on top of my head, it escalated then, his brothers got involved, his friends and then my friends, and it took off from there. It was driven by alcohol and tablets; there was no recollection of why it started. (P15)

Other feuds were sparked by more *commercial* motives, such as disagreements over drug territory or debts. Several participants described how the level of violence could gradually escalate and, at times, resulted in weapons being used:

> He shot one of these fellows, it nearly killed him, but he did not stop there ... they were knocking each other down off footpaths and hitting each other with slash hooks, it was a war. (P20)

> I was standing at a bus stop when fellas pulled up and let off a gun shot out the window. (P21)

Of course, participants were not only concerned about their public image if they failed to retaliate but also their own sense of self and self-respect, especially when group dynamics came into play. That is, they felt shame at not responding:

> If someone deliberately went out of their way to make a fool out of me, then there is a problem. If I don't act out then I am the mog, you should have done that nine times out of ten I used to lash out because it's better than listening to yourself. (P34)

Drink, Drugs and Doing Masculinity

For the men in this study, alcohol and drug consumption provided an avenue for building a reputation, gaining status and acceptance within their peer groups and the wider community. They spoke of taking drugs and drinking to excess as a means of being accepted by their peers and being seen as a man (also Carlsson, 2012; Darcy, 2020; Dolan, 2011; Dwyer, 2014); being able to ***hold your drink***, or drugs, was as important as holding your own in a fight. Drinking and drug use conformed to the type of masculinity the men wanted to portray, the type that was valued in their community. This type of identity formation linked to drug and alcohol consumption has long been recognised as a way of doing masculinity (Messerschmidt, 1993; also Dwyer, 2014), especially when intertwined with other valued behaviours:

> I felt like a man holding a can and drinking a naggin [200ml bottle] of vodka, it made me feel good, I could hold my drink. (P8)

> With that I started to get confidence started getting a reputation for the things I was doing on drink and drugs, robbing cars, houses. (P31)

With few legitimate opportunities to express their masculinity in a meaningful way, those learned behaviours and shared norms and values from the streets informed their sense of self and way of behaviour.

> I was a nice person, but my intentions were all wrong. I thought all that macho, trouble, drinking, even though I had a partner and kids, I thought you did not grow out of that. I never matured from the day I took a drink at 15, that macho persona came onto me. (P39)

Some reported being violent with or without alcohol; others used drink and/or drugs to find the courage to engage in violence. Some were even aware that they could not control their aggression while intoxicated so eventually avoided public spaces when under the influence. Most participants recalled getting involved in a lot of fights, and most incidents involved alcohol:

> It was always fighting, it was drink, whenever I had a drink and I went somewhere I always ended up fighting. (P17)

> The amount of fights I had after night clubs around town, and a lot of the times I would have put myself in dangerous situations where I would have been highly intoxicated on my own, fighting with crowds of people ... it was kind of in a black out, I was in a lot of emotional pain back then, a lot of suppressed anger and when I drank vodka and mixed tablets it came out I reckon. (P17)

Learning About Drink and Drugs

When they look back on their drug and alcohol use, many participants reflected on the role of intoxicants as a means of self-soothing—a way to dull psychological pain, or provide a level of self-assurance or confidence they felt was lacking. Most participants experimented with alcohol and drugs at a very young age, partly because they were surrounded by drug and alcohol misuse and addiction in the home and within the community, but also because they discovered very quickly the *benefits* of alcohol and drugs.

> When I found drink and drugs I really embraced that, I loved it. I was 13, it made me someone else, there was confidence there, it was a buzz. (P25)

There was even pressure from the community to become intoxicated. Many participants felt that people who did not drink alcohol or take drugs were outsiders.

> If you did not drink alcohol or smoke hash, it was abnormal like. (P15)

Such early exposure has often been identified as a risk factor for later problematic drug use (Kandel & Chen, 2000). One participant in this study reported how his group of friends, all of whom were experiencing problems at home, began sniffing solvents before they were 12 years old:

> I started using drugs in primary school, we would go on the hop [not attend school], we would rob bottles of nail varnish out of the shop, we'd get plastic bags and go sniffing nail varnish for the day. We were all the same age, similar situations as myself. Mad problems at home. (P31)

Addiction and Employment

A study by the Irish Probation Service (2012) linked 70 percent of crimes committed by individuals under the supervision of the probation service to the problematic use of alcohol or drugs. It noted that substance abuse often prevented individuals from earning money legitimately, so they turned to crime to finance their consumption. Some participants had never worked, some worked sporadically and some found that drinking and drug taking made staying in employment difficult. These themes were all present in the accounts of the participants in this study also.

Similar to the findings of the probation service, many participants in this study only engaged in acquisitive crime and/or drug dealing when they needed money to buy alcohol or drugs for their own use. Some reflected that they would never have committed a crime if not for their drink and drug addictions:

> I never committed a crime sober…The money that I got from crime went on drink and drugs. (P15)

However, others pointed to a lack of income as part of the problem. One participant pointed out that he would spend his salary on drinks and drugs, but once he lost his job, the cost of the addiction was met by shoplifting.

> When that [job] was gone I used to be getting into crime again, shoplifting to fund my drinking when my job was gone. (P17)

But for others, a macho culture had an impact on their perception of crime. One individual pointed out that being independent, and not reliant on others in the street for drugs and alcohol was a positive thing. He felt that having his own income, albeit an income derived from the proceeds of crime, was a positive achievement.

> I felt independent that I had money, that I could fund my own alcohol. (P32)

While unemployment has been identified as a risk factor for problematic drug consumption (Windle, 2018) some men identified being employed as contributing to heavy drinking and drug use. This was because they worked in jobs with big drinking and/or drug-taking cultures but also because a pay check meant they could temporarily afford alcohol and drugs. For example, P17, who started work as a teenager, was introduced to drinking by older men in a pub:

> It was like all my friends were down the field drinking cans and here am I in an early morning pub drinking with older men. I was the only fellow my age, there might have been 50 scaffolders worked for the company, they were all married men with children. It was just that area, the boom Celtic tiger, everything was just drink. (P17)

Some participants reported earning high wages in the building trade during the Celtic Tiger years. Heavy alcohol consumption was the norm at the time throughout Ireland and participants reported spending almost all of their wages on alcohol and drugs:

> I would have always had good money, which I would have blown, that was back in the boom, I was always broke from drink and smoking, no matter how much I had I was always broke on the Sunday. (P16)

The economic boom, and relatedly the high demand for manual labour particularly in the building trade, alongside good wages did prevent some of the participants from engaging in acquisitive crimes. For example, upon release from prison, P14 had planned a return to crime as a means of funding his lifestyle but found a well-paying job instead. At the time, the salaries in construction had skyrocketed and some of the men were able to provide for their families.

> I got out in 2000, I got a job. I came out with the intentions of getting involved in crime that time, I did not, I was getting the bones of €1600 a week, I was [thinking] fuck this, this is great, it was different, I was different. (P14)

> At the time I was bringing in €600 to a €1000 a week, we thought it would never end, life was great. We had loads of money. Take the kids down every Saturday for tracksuits and runners, they always had the best bikes, they had everything they wanted, stuff I never had as a kid. (P13)

The unsustainable salaries of the Celtic tiger era disappeared with the 2008 crash of the construction industry and the economy more generally. Unskilled roles were the first jobs to go once the recession happened.

> I was involved in crime again. 2008, 2009, 2010 I was locked up. Everything went balls up; the building trade was gone also. (P14)

> Did you go straight back to crime? (Graham)

> Yah, when you are used to the money, you could not do without it. (P14)

Some participants link their decline into addiction as directly related to a lack of employment and a lack of a good salary. For example, the economic crash put P13 on a downward spiral. He started consuming more alcohol, which strained family relationships and he left the family home:

> Well I lost the job in 2008, the building trade went sour. So as I was not working, I started drinking more, which was not good, we started arguing in front of the kids which was not good. I ended up walking out, I started to go downhill from then, 2009 and on, up to 2013 were the dark days in my life. (P13)

For others, however, the spiral into addiction happened in spite of the well-paying job, and as such the salary was an insufficient barrier to addiction. The men reflected that they spent almost all of their wages on alcohol and drugs and, as their consumption increased, they began to lose control, turning up to work under the influence, or not turning up at all:

> I was exploring with tablets; I was taking them 10, 20, 30s. When you have someone coming onto a [building] site in a dangerous area out of my bin, they had no other choice to send me home. (P33)

> Once I get paid I would not turn up after I got my pay packet, I would go on a mad one and I would not turn up, I would be there for a day or two, and then I would be gone for that. (P27)

> The job was ok for a while but then it became drinking Thursday till Tuesday, there was periods where I would miss Monday and Tuesday ringing in sick. Everyone knew I was a drinker that I was fighting all the time. (P30)

While the experience of addiction was a very personal journey, the undulations of the national and global economy had very real consequences for those individuals at the mercy of unskilled and precarious employment. Some only began engaging in acquisitive crime in an effort to feed their addiction once the economy entered a downturn. For others, the salaries of the Celtic Tiger provided a temporary buffer that prevented their problems from bubbling to the surface. For others, having money made their situation worse and quickened their progression into addiction (see Bruguera et al., 2018). In short, changes to the global and local economy impacted individuals differently: being employed triggered some, not being employed triggered others.

Losing Control: The Descent into Addiction

Based on the data analysis in this study, there were clusters of themes that accounted for the commonalities in the way the men understood the role of addiction in their lives. The men spoke about the functional role of drink and drugs, including self-soothing, masking trauma, providing a release from their day-to-day problems, relieving boredom, as a means of bonding with friends, assisting in the development of a hyper masculine identity and bolstering self-esteem.

However, this *functionality* was short lived, and while the substances served a purpose in the beginning, for the men in this study, the drugs and alcohol soon became the focus as they entered active addiction. The men found themselves seeking out alcohol and drugs, not for the functional reasons described above, but to overcome the hangovers, and to avoid the emotional cliff that comes with addiction. All of the men eventually became physically and emotionally dependent on drugs and/or alcohol.

The men described the move from the early days of *social using*, to problematic usage. This involved consuming while alone, chaotic and risky behaviours while intoxicated and ultimately addiction and total dependence. At this stage, the men began to disengage from family, education, employment and most activities they had previously enjoyed. The behaviours that the men sought to bolster via drugs and alcohol use—namely aggression, violence and sociability—became the behaviours they could not control and sought to hide from. Ironically for the men, taking alcohol and drugs—once a tool to reinforce their masculinity—had become the very thing that stripped them of the valued ***hard-man*** identity. Alcohol and drugs were no longer serving to soothe past traumas but were generating new problems and traumas. At this point, the substance became the means and the end:

> I was always thinking about tomorrow, I suppose fear of not having something [drugs] in me, to get away from me, I would wake up and I would want a drink or a tablet. I was never sober, it was madness really. (P10)

The drink and drugs eventually overtook all other social activities that they had been interested in:

> I knew nothing at the time, I suppose school was out the window, Fr Horrigan's boxing was gone, the basketball was gone, just wanting to do nothing, just get stoned and drunk. (P10)

Many men became isolated. Some were fearful of how they behaved when intoxicated, so began avoiding going out in public:

> I used never go out I used to be too terrified to go to the clubs because of who I would meet, I knew I would end up fighting. (P16)

P16's quote indicates how taking drugs or drinking alone had become more important than socialising and having fun—predominantly due to a lack of control. In addition, many men lost the capacity to look after their health and well-being as their addiction progressed; ultimately the substances that had initially served to numb psychological pain, act as a social buffer and facilitate group belonging, had become a tool of self-harm:

> I was empty reaching [vomiting] every morning for years. Very hard to put food inside me, so you could say, I was malnourished because of drink. (P23)

> I remember my first night in the cell I started to get desperate nose bleeds, I was after taking cocaine for months and drinking heavy and then all of a

> sudden I was withdrawn, then I started to panic because I had nothing in the cell, the cell was bare not a sup of water, and I was going through the rats from the drink, lying in bed and the blood pouring out of my nose. I taught I was going to die that night. (P17)

Loss of Control: Addiction, Crime and Problem Behaviours

The men reported frequently losing control while intoxicated. It was not unusual for them to wake up in Gardaí cells after a night of drinking and/or drug taking (see Leonard, 2021). Participants recalled how, on the walk home from the station, they would often plan to give up alcohol or drugs. But the thought was often short-lived as instead, they decided to have a quick pint, a joint, or a couple of bets at the bookies. Sometimes, however, they would stop but only to substitute one drug with another, jumping from one addiction to another (see Sussman & Black, 2008):

> I would go on benders, I would come back to the house, and I would tell myself this is the end of it. I did not know it at the time but I was powerless to the disease. I wanted to stop but I could not stop. I could stop certain things, if I stopped the drinking, I would substitute it for the weed [cannabis], if I had no money for the weed I would go back to the drink. I would find a cheaper route not to deal with life. (P37)

For P14, desisting from crime resulted in increased drug consumption and eventual addiction. He describes using drugs to replace the thrill of involvement in crime, although the new high seldom lasted very long:

> There is no comparison at all, crime is the thing, well it was the thing for me. I never felt everything…I'll take drugs, because I am not doing crime, it's a fucked up way to look at it but if I was not involved in crime, I would not be involved in drugs. (P14)

This idea of chasing a high and/or thrill through any kind of risk-taking behaviour emerged as a theme across the interviews. For example, one participant, who was in recovery from problematic drug use, decided that he would gamble a little each week. He justified this by thinking there was no harm if he could limit himself to a €10 bet a week, however, he quickly relapsed:

> I convinced myself that I could have a bet on the soccer, that I was not using [drugs or alcohol], my life is falling into place, just spend €10 every week. I learned through experience that I can't have a bet. (P32)

His gambling got worse, he lost any ability to control his gambling and eventually it became emotionally and financially harmful. He responded in the only way he knew: by returning to alcohol to cope and soothe the pain.

> It snowballed again, and I ended up drinking again. (P32)

For the participants in this study, the issue was not a particular substance or behaviour, but the need to *treat* the impact of current and past problems in their lives. Ultimately this *self-medicating* became a problem in its own right, and the men slipped into addiction. The addiction caused more trauma, more guilt, more relationship breakdowns and more abuse and so the cycle of addiction and relapse continued. In short, when participants chose to stop consuming they lost their primary mechanism for coping with life, both past and present—drink and drugs may not be particularly good ways of coping long term, but they were often the only ones available to the men at the time.

Loss of Control: Denial, Isolation and a Shattered Identity

The academic literature suggests that individuals with addiction issues also present with other mental health disorders (Brannigan et al., 2004): most commonly, depressive and anxiety disorders, social phobia, PTSD, conduct disorders, and oppositional defiant disorder (Abrantes et al., 2004). Importantly causality is not one way—mental health disorders do not *cause* addiction (and vice versa) in some unidirectional fashion and, the lifestyle and history of individuals play significant roles in the emergence of mental ill health. In this study, such co-morbidity was routinely mentioned, the origins of which often lay in the personal and social history of the men. Years of active addiction played havoc with the men's self-esteem, confidence, relationships and identity, particularly their sense of masculinity. Their identity, their sense of what it meant to be a man, was shattered by the effects of their lifestyle: the drink and drugs eventually sapped them off their physicality. They could no longer fight. To deal with these emotions, the men turned to their key coping strategy; they took more drinks or drugs, which, of course, only worsened their physical and mental health.

At this stage, many participants saw no way out. In their eyes, suicide was often their only viable option. Some of the men attempted suicide multiple times. Others self-medicated with increasingly larger doses of drugs/alcohol in the hope that it would take away the anguish they were feeling and, if not, that they would die from an overdose.

The problems in their lives accumulated the longer they were in active addiction. It was not unusual for participants to lose their families before they realised how bad things were. P36 recalled pushing everyone out of his life:

> I now know it was a bad experience for me, my addiction. I got divorced, I lost my kids, drink took over my life. I had to be miserable, push everyone away, my family, and my children. I never loved anyone, because I never loved myself. I pushed everyone away, I lived miserable, and I thought I would die miserable also. (P36)

P30 discussed the strain that his addiction placed on his pregnant partner and his parents:

> There was a lot of pressures from herself because she was pregnant. I was fighting all the time, there was lots of arguments at home with my parents. I was liable to go missing on the weekends. Because I could not stop drinking. (P30)

While participants were able to identify that their addiction was causing significant harm to them and those closest to them, stopping was far from simple. The men were self-medicating with alcohol and drugs. They were trying to overcome trauma, psychological illness, identity issues and peer pressure. Removing the substances, which were their (poorly conceived) coping strategies, bought these issues to the fore. The realisation of having to deal with a lifetime of psychological problems in a more meaningful way, without drugs and alcohol as a crutch was a difficult realisation for the men (see Fisher, 2000).

In addition to mental and physical health issues, the progression of their addiction also resulted in them committing more crimes to pay for more drugs and alcohol. This increased offending was also a consequence of their behaviour becoming more erratic:

> I hated everyone and everything. My using around that time started to change... selling drugs instead of getting an ounce, I would get a bar, then the hundreds of tablets everything started to escalate, and as a result there was bigger consequences, bigger debts, fighting with people all the time. (P19)

> Was your alcohol and drug use getting worse, when you started to do these robberies? (Graham)

> My addiction progressed at the age of 15 ...It went from shoplifting to robbing cars committing burglaries at age 15. (P32)

P32 was facing an extended prison sentence for drug dealing. The consequence of incarceration was not enough to stop him from continuing this behaviour. Ultimately, it was spending time in a treatment centre, rather than prison, which helped him desist. The addiction was the root of everything and without addressing it, nothing else could improve. The threat of prison was not going to force or help him to leave addiction behind:

> I was getting worse and worse, where you have a couple of sentences behind you, you would think, now I am not doing this anymore, but no I was getting worse up till the time I went to treatment. (P27)

Despite most participants having received a number of prison sentences, they were not deterred from consuming alcohol or drugs, nor engaging in crime (also Leonard, 2021; Leonard & Windle, 2020). The worse their addiction became the greater the realisation that they were losing control of their life, sense of self, social identity and mental health. The public hard-man identity was slipping away due to the progression of their addiction.

> I was shattered, that is why I felt so lost like, I was left with myself, and I could not keep up the front anymore, I was bait [exhausted] from the alcohol and the drugs at the time. (P16)

Narrative approaches to social psychology shed light on the experience of losing one's sense of self, they explain how we have ideas of who we are and what our lives are about (McAdams, 2001) and how important it is to be able to tell a coherent story about who we are. This portrayed or public identity is important to our sense of self it influences our activities, inspirations and choices while providing our lives with meaning (Maruna, 2001). Importantly it also justifies past behaviour and reconciles our past with our present. Addiction significantly impacts self-identity: it chips away at the men's sense of who they are while preventing them from upholding the alternative identities they value. Participants prioritised the need to portray themselves as tough, to project fear and be intimidating. This was not only important for survival but was a culturally approved norm. As such, the men felt that this identity was the only one available to them, but as their addiction progressed, they lost control of their ability to project this identity and so lost this valued sense of self.

Ironically excessive drugs/alcohol consumption, behaviours that initially bolstered that hard-man identity, ultimately eroded it. This is because years of substance abuse prevented them from being able to project the type of masculinity they valued. Consequently, many men were simultaneously experiencing both active addiction and an existential crisis of identity (DuPont & McGovern, 1992; Farrall, 2005):

> The older people I looked up to were all gone, they settled down, they could control their drinking, they had kids and they got older, then the younger crowd came through. I started being around them around the corners, it was only pity, I was a pity, I was falling around the place, and they were looking after me, 7 years younger. I ended up going from being respected around the place, to people saying for fuck sake here is again. (P39)

As P39 was now unable to defend himself, he was left open to victimisation and was assaulted several times:

> I would be falling around the place, at this stage, I would have got a good few beatings while drinking. (P39)

This went on for three years. At the end of which he felt 'broken':

> Home was non-existent, I petered out, I became a loner, I just saluted people, I never felt wanted. I was broking mental and physically. (P39)

Most participants told similar stories: the longer they were problematically using alcohol and drugs, the worse life became for them, on every front. For some, the only refuge was prison or a treatment centre. Going to either of these places did not, however, guarantee recovery from their addiction, but offered a break, a timeout, from the chaos of their lives.

The consequences of their lifestyle—the prison, violence, estranged families and traumatic experiences—led some participants to turn in on themselves. They started to resent and hate the person they had become. One participant hated himself so much that they would break mirrors to prevent this 'other' person looking back at him:

> I did not like me, I self-harmed myself an awful lot, I did not like looking into a mirror, every mirror I looked into I broke it. I hated myself big time, it is frighten when you think back though, not wanting to live, in and out of prison, and knowing nothing. (P10)

Many dealt with these emotions by taking more drugs. This caused a further deterioration in their mental health which, in turn, prevented them from dealing with their problems in a healthy or effective way:

> I became very paranoid on it, I did not know was it paranoia or reality. I could smoke a joint of hash and the paranoia would come on again. Yet I still was smoking it still taking it because I could not live with myself, could not sit with myself, I could not deal with emotions, so I had to take these things. (P39)

Some found their brief periods without drink or drugs very difficult. For example, P39 found being a father emotionally challenging. He tried to cope with day-to-day life as a parent by again turning to substances as a means of coping, but it inevitably made things worse. For many of the men, the experience of trauma and harm was a key part of their addiction, but in addition, the lack of coping skills necessary to deal with day-to-day life was also a factor. This participant pointed out that he did not have the skills to cope with life's routine challenges:

> When I was not on these things, I was paranoid. I would say I am never going to take these things again, I don't want to take these things again. Then the minute I would come down I would have to deal with emotions, deal with my family, being a dad. I could not deal with that, I suppose I was caught between a rock and a hard place, for years. It made me very sick, physically and mentally. (P39)

For all participants, when the substances they used to cope with life failed to soothe their current emotional pain, their mental health suffered. Some accelerated their drug or alcohol consumption in an effort to numb the emotional pain. The more they consumed, however, the worse their mental health got.

The deterioration of participants' mental health, and their increasing addiction, left them feeling isolated. They could not talk to peers about their feelings as any discussion of emotions was contrary to the valued hard-man identity; displays of such emotions were seen as a sign of weakness. Despite their suffering, participants remained concerned with maintaining the hard-man image:

> When you are trying to live up to this macho image it is hard, you are not letting people in to what is really going on what is inside your head. (P9)

Loss of Control: Suicide, Self-Harm and Death

As mentioned, suicide often featured in the life experiences of the participants. All of the men in this study had friends or family members who had died from suicide often via drug overdose. They had all experienced near-death episodes themselves. Twelve of the 40 participants reported having attempted suicide and a further seven reported suicidal thoughts. Most reported deliberate or accidental overdoses as well as other forms of or self-harm.[1] Some examples provided by the men included:

> He lost the plot, he then grabbed tablets out of a drawer, there was a steroid in them, he took 20 of them, over the next 24 hours he got 15 cardiac arrest and he died at 19. (P21)

> One drowned off the Shaky Bridge (a Cork landmark), and another died in a robed car. (P15)

> A friend of mine he is dead now he committed suicide last year. (P19)

> There was a friend of mine going to NA, he is dead now - overdosed with a needle in his arm in a toilet in town. (P25)

[1] Ireland has the third highest rate of drug-related deaths in Europe: 70.5 drug deaths per million people, compared with an EU average of 17.1 per million. This is almost double the UK average (EMCDDA, 2014).

> A good friend of mine that was with me, who is in recovery now also, he gave me mouth to mouth, rang an ambulance. I had to be resuscitated with the defibrillators, I remember coming around and there was ambulance and flashing lights on my way to the Mercy (hospital) I died again, they had to resuscitate me again. (P32)

Overdose, suicide and even murder were not uncommon experiences for the men. One participant describes using drugs to try to cope with the grief.

> Since I lost that friend, I have lost a lot of other friends over overdose, suicide, one was murdered, I think death became an occupational hazard after a while the funerals got easier to go to, not that they were easy to go to, but I did not feel as much, now I was using more drugs and the drugs that I was using was the ultimate pain killer. (P25)

The men also spoke about their own attempts at suicide. They describe it as a release, and as the only option available to them. They saw it as the best–worst-option—they referenced the harm they *might* do to others, and described thinking suicide would save them and others from this fate.

> I was going to overdose, my body was just going to shut down I was either going to kill someone or myself, I suppose my head was just gone. (P17)

> I can remember being 17 and wanted to take my life, and I did, I through myself off Patrick's Bridge one night like, fucking three o'clock in the morning, in the middle of January, just like a switch, my head told me and bang. (P10)

The men also spoke about being fatalistic about their drug use, knowing the harm they were doing to their minds and bodies, and hoping that they might die while intoxicated. P10 continued to experience suicidal ideation for years, often hoping that he would die from an overdose:

> I was sick of being sick, I was going nowhere in life, and wanting to die for years, I can remember drinking a bottle of whiskey and taking tablets many of a night and saying take me please. (P10)

P15 discussed consuming a large amount of heroin, knowing that it would either stop the depression or kill him, and he did not care which:

> I was drunk, I had two €25 bags of heroin and I put them onto the spoon, I know now that this was too much, but I was drunk, emotional and depressed, I just taught this is going to make me not depressed or its going to kill me, but I did not care, it would take me out of the way I was feeling at that moment, I injected it, I overdosed immediately. So the needle was still in my arm and I woke up and two paramedics and two Gardaí were standing over me. (P15)

Others considered suicide because they felt it was the only way to end their addiction, they saw no other way out, no other way to get help or help themselves:

> Continued using, I suppose it was till I was 28 to 31 that I really wanted to stop using but I did not know how. That's how the attempts on my life [happened]. (P32)

The tragic situations that led to the men attempting suicide were antagonised by the physical and mental impact of the event. Overdoses and suicide attempts had long-term impacts on many participants' health:

> I was so fucked from that overdose... Ya, I could not go outside the door, I was so sick in my head I used to get violent headaches, body tremors. (P17)

> That is why I think I have epilepsy today. (P13)

The men were around death: they had friends and family who died early, and they all knew people who had attempted suicide. They coped with grief in the only way they knew: by consuming more drink and drugs, which exacerbated their mental and physical health problems.

Prison: Identity Shifts and Self-Reflection

Prison was a constant presence for all the men in this study: not only did going in and out of prison became the norm, but so too did visiting incarcerated family and friends, and gossiping about those who had been imprisoned, or were due to be imprisoned. Most participants were imprisoned at least once while in active addiction. This was often a consequence of committing crimes to finance consumption but also acts of violence and aggression committed while intoxicated.

Going to prison served a number of purposes for the men, depending on the life stage they were at. For some, especially in their youth, it was something that was highly anticipated as a rite of passage. It bolstered their hard-man image, providing near-celebrity status amongst their peers and the young people in their area. The men, when they were boys, talked amongst themselves about the prison, the cells and wings, who was in control in the prison, who they looked up to in prison and used prison *knowledge* and contacts as a form of social capital. For others, at other stages of their lives, prison served a particular function, it saved them from themselves, and in many cases from death: they saw prison as a blessing in disguise. The men reflect that they may not have realised this at the time, but it gave them respite from a chaotic life that was slowly killing them. For others in this study, as they got older, they realised prison offered time to assess where their lives were going and reflect on how to move away from their problematic lifestyle. Some identified the services available in prison, especially addiction and educational services, as having a positive impact. This said, many recalled that as soon as they left the prison, often after a successful period of abstinence, they very quickly returned to problematic drug and alcohol consumption. This was often due to a return to their community, a reengagement with problematic peers and a lack of support services outside of the prison.

Most participants in this study had repeat convictions and multiple stays in prison. This is to be expected as the recidivism rate for offenders in Ireland is 62.3 percent (Irish Prison Service, 2013). For this particular group, the role of early engagement with the criminal justice system was significant because the literature has demonstrated that individuals who begin offending as children are more likely to be persisters than desisters (Blokland & Palmen, 2012).

All of the participants in this study experienced prison differently and each sentence served was differently. How they experienced incarceration depended on the state of their active addiction, their family situation, their physical and mental health, and their age: young men may use prison as a space to build social capital, while the same man may later use prison to gain an education, learn about himself or as a first step into rehabilitation.

At a community level, for these men, the prison held a place in the lore of the community. Older lads from the area would tell stories of their escapades in prison, often reminiscing about their experiences. This made prison seem attractive to the young boys who were captivated by the stories and impressed by the status attained by the older men due to their reputation, they looked up to the men as role models.

> I remember being up there [prison], there was a bit of curiosity, because you would hear older lads talking about it. I do not know what it was but I wanted to know what they were on about, what it was like. There was always a fascination with it. I wanted to see it. (P30)

> How you would have to piss in the cell, how you bring in drugs, stories of the yard, the fighting, the cutting up, it was all attractive. I was attracted to madness. (P39)

While the reality of prison did initially frighten most participants, they quickly started to relax- this was because they realised that they 'fit in'. The men in the prison mostly came from the same part of the city (see Leonard, 2021; O'Donnell et al., 2007; O'Mahony, 2003)[2] and they shared a similar culture and often a similar view on life. Most reported that they were not too bored with prison, and adapted quickly. The ability to cope with prison made return visits less overwhelming—the men knew what to expect:

> Yes there was always someone you knew, I can't remember being in there with someone I did not know. (P27)

> I fitted in there, I felt I belonged in there. I was with people who were taking drugs and had the same ideology as me. It was very easy for me to blend in there, playing handball, playing football, go to the school, fall into that routine, it was grand. (P15)

> It was a badge of honour......when they come out their like 'I am the man and look at me'. (P9)

[2] A study which analysed the address details of 5588 people released from Irish prisons during 2004 found that Irish prisoners are 23 times more likely to come from (and return to) seriously economically deprived areas (O'Donnell et al., 2007).

Knowing so many people within the prison presented additional complications. There was no escape from the problematic dynamics of the communities the men came from, there was always a concern with saving face and maintaining the hard-man identity. This preoccupation with demonstrating a particular type of masculinity was a barrier for the men—it prevented them from engaging in intervention programmes in the prison. Given that the structures of the community were often replicated inside the prison, it was difficult to leave their outside life behind. Conflicts and feuds followed them from the streets into the prison where fighting and feuding were common:

> I went to Cork prison first, but I was in a spot of bother, a fellow tried to stab me in the throat with a scissors. I did not know who he was..... I had some argument with his son. (P21)

While prison could potentially offer respite for some individuals, for others it merely transplanted the dynamics from the street into the more intense prison environment (Mitchell et al., 2017); fear, intimidation and violence remained necessary survival strategies in the prison. Indeed, portraying the hard-man image remained a means of avoiding being the victim of violence or bullying (see Kupers, 2005):

> Did you still have to go in there with the hard-man image? (Graham)

> Well you have to keep it up, because if they think you are … not hard they would walk all over you, you would be picked out and bullied, or made an eejit out of. (P31)

The men felt that there was little difference between how you should carry yourself within the prison and in their communities:

> It is the same kind of environment, it's all image and front and you have this wall in front of you, where no one sees you as weak, and it is all street talk, and street attitude, and street rules, it is very similar, coming from the area I was on the outside coming to prison it was very similar situations, very similar ideologies, ways of seeing society. (P15)

Consistent with Anderson's (1999) street code, P21 identified how people bullied others as a means of building their own image. The participant also talked of the importance of understanding the prison hierarchy, and the violence arising from the drugs trade:

> You would never see the top dogs doing anything, it is always the fellas underneath them. It always over drugs and stuff and money. (P21)

Despite these issues, for some of the men in this study, prison provided a space for respite from their chaotic lives on the outside. P15, for example, talked of 'not caring' if he was arrested, because he would at least escape from the chaos of his daily life:

> Because sometimes prison was the best place for me, a good few times I went to prison and I was on deaths door, and prison was a breather from the madness. (P15)

In a reflection of the hardship and trauma experienced by some of the men in this study, one participant recalled how being sent to prison as a child meant he would at least have food and shelter. For P36, prison also gave him a break from being violently attacked on the streets.

> I went in to prison when I was 15 for drink driving no insurance, went in there I thought it was the best thing, because I did not have to run any more. I was not getting beatings, I went in there I had food; I had a roof over my head. (P36)

For some of the men in this study, prison was an opportunity to take time out from their chaotic lives. That is, their lives were so difficult, that the stability and relative safety of prison felt like a reprieve. Prison also provided the opportunity to avoid alcohol and drugs for a period of time, and even engage with support services. This was short-lived, however, because they often quickly regressed upon release. P26 felt that prison was easier than life on the outside:

> Prison is alright, when you are in addiction, your sentence starts when you get out, for me I start battling my demons when I got out, when I was in there I feel safe, and comfortable. (P26)

Prison was a second chance for some participants and prevented premature death:

> If I pick up a drink and I end up in prison I would be very lucky. Locked away again and maybe get another chance at it. Because if I continue, there might be no coming back... I would probably top myself, or die slowly. (P10)

In some instances, once in prison, the men could reflect on their lives. With the option for alcohol and drug use limited, they had space to think. One participant spoke about how, while he was in prison, his family came back into his life. He had become a father for the first time, which gave him the motivation to start confronting the chaos he was living with:

> The first three months was just staying in my cell doing nothing else, sitting around thinking what I was doing with my life, where I was after ending up, but it was the best experience in my life, where it's got me clean, my family came back around me, my partner, I did not like the thought of my child being brought in there because he was a few weeks old, but it gave me the motivation to sort myself out. (P12)

Some were able to stay away from alcohol and drugs while incarcerated and reported starting to feel healthier. This gave them the distance, clarity, the physical and emotional strength to reflect on their lives. It also provided some with a well-needed boost to their self-esteem, or as P3s put it:

> It gets the brain thinking right again. (P3)

P13 also 'sobered up' in prison, and reflected with a new clarity on his situation. Realising that he was not a young man motivated him to access treatment within the prison:

> When I got to the jail, I sobered up and started thinking about everything, and started to see that this was not healthy, I have to do something about this, I was 40 years of age and I was going around like a teenager. (P13)

Once participants realized that they wanted to stop, and were open to change, they had access to the necessary supports in prison. Most reported a positive experience with prison support workers, and that they made steps in the right direction. This said, release often served to disrupt their rehabilitation and many returned to old habits due to issues including reengaging with peer networks and individuals seeking to spoil their recovery, lack of access to services, problems with housing and lack of employment. These are all issues that will be discussed in the next chapter.

Conclusion

A number of themes were discussed in this chapter. Key amongst them was the social identity that was *necessary* to survive on the streets and in prison and the value system that supported the prioritisation of this identity. Demonstrating a hard-man image within their community (and by extension prison) was the norm. The men in this study learned at a young age the necessity of portraying this image through violence or the threat of violence, by retaliating against any perceived insult and showing they could 'look after themselves'. Failing to demonstrate this particular type of masculinity could result in victimisation. The protective function of this image aside, the men sought the power and status afforded in their community by being seen as a hard man. Drinking large amounts of alcohol and taking large amounts of illicit drugs was also integral to forming, and maintaining, the hard-man image. Drink and drug consumption also served to soothe and calm the emotional pain of childhood and adult trauma. That is, heavy alcohol and drug use served a number of cultural and psychological purposes. They were central to surviving in tough environments and coping with significant trauma.

For the men in this study, however, their alcohol and drug use progressed to a point whereby it became uncontrolled and they eventually became addicted. Their consumption started to harm their mental and physical health, education, employment opportunities and disrupt any healthy relationships they had. Overdoses and suicide were omnipresent in their lives, and in the lives of their peers, drugs and alcohol became less useful and rather than serving specific social and psychological functions, substances served only to alleviate the symptoms of withdrawal. Ultimately the substances that originally assisted in the individual achieving social status, power and a hard-man identity led to the dissolution of everything they valued. The substance use began to cause more trauma, which could then only be soothed by more alcohol and more drugs. Addiction broke down any pro-social relationships the men had, it reduced the participant's physicality and they lost the identity they had craved since childhood. Ultimately, they lost the most valued aspect of their sense of self, their hard-man image.

Prison also served a purpose for the men, along the same lines as the use of drugs and willingness to use violence. As young men it allowed them to form and refine the hard-man image, to boost their local status and reputation. As they got older, and their addiction progressed, prison (alongside treatment centres and psychiatric units for some) provided the only break from their chaotic lives. Within these institutions, participants could get clarity on where their lives were going and enabled them to make plans to change. While some succeeded, others relapsed numerous times, but these institutions often kept them alive, exposed them to support and provided a break from the chaos of the streets. It gave them a chance to think, to breathe.

That is of course not to say that the prison experience is all positive, or that Irish prisons are free of drugs (see Dillon, 2001). Rather, for the men in this study, when they retrospectively reflected on their journey out of addiction and crime, they constructed prison as predominantly a positive experience in their recovery journey. Indeed, prison allowed them to start 'active engagement in the process of identity reconstruction' towards a 'new self' (Crewe & Levins, 2019: 1). For some, prison was the beginning of a long road, which is where the next chapter turns.

References

Abrantes, A. M., Brown, S. A., & Tomlinson, K. L. (2004). Psychiatric comorbidity among inpatient substance abusing adolescents. *Journal of Child and Adolescent Substance Abuse, 13*(2), 83–101.

Anderson, E. (1999). *Code of the street: Decency, violence, and the moral life of the inner city*. Norton.

Blokland, A. A., & Palmen, H. (2012). Criminal career patterns. In R. Loeber, M. Hoeve, N. W. Slot, & P. van der Laan (Eds.), *Persisters and desisters in crime from adolescence into adulthood* (pp. 13–50). Routledge.

Brannigan, R., Schackman, B. R., Falco, M., & Millman, R. B. (2004). The quality of highly regarded adolescent substance abuse treatment programs: Results of an in-depth national survey. *Archives of Paediatrics and Adolescent Medicine, 158*(4), 904–909.

Bruguera, P., Reynolds, J., Gilvarry, E., Braddick, F., Marath-Veettil, A. L., Anderson, P., & Gual, A. (2018). How does economic recession affect substance use? A reality check with clients of drug treatment centres. *The Journal of Mental Health Policy and Economics, 21*(1), 11–16.

Carlsson, C. (2012). Using 'turning points' to understand processes of change in offending: Notes from a Swedish study on life courses and crime. *The British Journal of Criminology, 52*(1), 1–16.

Connell, R. (2005). *Masculinities*. Polity.

Connell, R. W., & Messerschmidt, J. W. (2005). Hegemonic masculinity: Rethinking the concept. *Gender and Society, 19*(6), 829–859.

Crewe, B., & Levins, A. (2019). The prison as a reinventive institution. *Theoretical Criminology, 24*(4), 568–589.

Darcy, C. (2020). Men and the drug buzz: Masculinity and men's motivations for illicit recreational drug use. *Sociological Research Online, 25*(3), 421–437.

Dillon, L. (2001). *Drug use among prisoners: An exploratory study*. The Health Research Board.

Dolan, A. (2011). 'You can't ask for a Dubonnet and lemonade!': Working class masculinity and men's health practices. *Sociology of Health and Illness, 33*(4), 586–601.

DuPont, R. L., & McGovern, J. P. (1992). Suffering in addiction: Alcoholism and drug dependence. In P. L. Starck & J. P. McGovern (Eds.), *The hidden dimension of illness: Human suffering* (pp. 155–201). National League for Nursing Press.

Dwyer, D. (2014). The lived experiences of men in 12-step recovery against a backdrop of hegemonic masculinity. *Irish Probation Journal, 11*(1), 177–195.

EMCDDA (European Monitoring Centre for Drugs and Drug Addiction). (2014). *European drug report (2014)*. http://www.emcdda.europa.eu/edr 2014

Farrall, S. (2005). On the existential aspects of desistance from crime. *Symbolic Interaction, 28*(3), 367–386.

Fisher, J. (2000). Addictions and trauma recovery. *Paper presented at the International Society for the Study of Dissociation*. https://janinafisher.com/pdfs/addictions.pdf

Goffman, E. (1967). *Interaction ritual: Essays on face-to-face interaction*. Aldine.Graham, H. (2016). *Rehabilitation work: Supporting desistance and recovery*. Routledge.

Gunter, A. (2017). *Race, gangs and youth violence: Policy, prevention and policing*. Policy Press.

Hourigan, N., Morrison, J. F., Windle, J., & Silke, A. (2018). Crime in Ireland north and south: Feuding gangs and profiteering paramilitaries. *Trends in Organized Crime, 21*(2), 126–146.

Irish Prison Service. (2013). *Irish prison service recidivism study*. https://www.irishprisons.ie/images/pdf/recidivismstudyss2.pdf

Kandel, D., & Chen, K. (2000). Types of marijuana users by longitudinal course. *Journal of Studies on Alcohol, 61*(3), 367–378.

Katz, J. (1988). *Seductions of crime*. Basic Books.

Kupers, T. A. (2005). Toxic masculinity as a barrier to mental health treatment in prison. *Journal of Clinical Psychology, 61*(6), 713–724.

Leonard, J. (2021). An autobiographical account of desistance and recovery. In Lynch, O., Windle, J., & Ahmed, Y. (Eds.), *Giving voice to diversity in criminological research: Nothing about us without us* (pp. 149–156). Policy.

Leonard, J., & Windle, J. (2020). 'I could have went down a different path': Talking to people who used drugs problematically and service providers about Irish drug policy alternatives. *International Journal of Drug Policy, 84*, 102891.

Maruna, S. (2001). *Making good: How ex-convicts reform and rebuild their lives*. American Psychological Association Press.

McAdams, D. P. (2001). The psychology of life stories. *Review of General Psychology, 5*(2), 100–122.

Messerschmidt, J. (1993). *Masculinities and crime*. Rowman and Littlefield.

Mitchell, M. M., Fahmy, C., Pyrooz, D. C., & Decker, S. H. (2017). Criminal crews, codes, and contexts: Differences and similarities across the code of the street, convict code, street gangs, and prison gangs. *Deviant Behaviour, 38*(10), 1197–1222.

Mullins, C. W. (2006). *Holding your square: Masculinities, streetlife and violence*. Willan.

O'Donnell, I., Teljeur, C., Hughes, N., Baumer, E., & Kelly, A. (2007). When prisoners go home: Punishment, social deprivation and the geography of reintegration. *Irish Criminal Law Journal, 17*(4), 3–9.

O'Mahony, P. (2003). *Criminal Justice in Ireland*. Institute of Public Administration.

Probation Service. (2012). *Drug and alcohol misuse among adult offenders on probation supervision in Ireland*. Probation Service.

Sussman, S., & Black, D. S. (2008). Substitute addiction: A concern for researchers and practitioners. *Journal of Drug Education, 38*(2), 167–180.

Willis, P. (1977). *Learning to labour. How working class kids get working class jobs*. Routledge.

Windle, J. (2018). The impact of the Great Recession on the Irish drug market. *Criminology and Criminal Justice, 18*(5), 548–567.

Windle, J. (2019). The causes and consequences of gangland violence in the Republic of Ireland. In R. Lombardo (Ed.), *Organized crime: Causes and consequences* (pp. 110–123). Nova Science.

Windle, J., & Briggs, D. (2015). Going solo: The social organisation of drug dealing within a London street gang. *Journal of Youth Studies, 18*(9), 1170–1185.

Windle, J., Moyle, L., & Coomber, R. (2020). 'Vulnerable' kids going country: Children and young people's involvement in county lines drug dealing. *Youth Justice, 20*(1–2), 64–78.

CHAPTER 7

Moving Out of the Chaos

Abstract This final results chapter recounts the themes that explain desistance and recovery for the men who participated in this study. Key overarching themes include cycles of relapse, identity shifts, a lack of alternatives, new starts, difficult transitions (prison to community), the social nature of recovery and maintaining a new life. Throughout all of these themes was the necessity for a global life shift—the need to fully and comprehensively embrace a new life, an honest life in order to succeed long term. This shift was complicated by family relationships and peer networks and this chapter presents the findings on how this issue was navigated by the participants in this study. Finally, this chapter addresses the issue of the emergence and evolution of a new identity, how maturity is relevant for this process and how the men reflect on their journey to date.

Keywords Relapse · Identity shift · Transition · Living a good life

This chapter recounts participants' accounts as they talk of attempting recovery and desistance. The men's journeys were, in many cases, marked by multiple false starts, relapses and repeated ***rock bottoms***. The men all described reaching rock bottom—while this term has been criticised as

G. Cambridge et al., *The Desistance Journey*,
https://doi.org/10.1007/978-3-031-11269-0_7

stigmatising, it is the phrase the men themselves used and was important to them. Rock bottom has been defined by DuPont and McGovern (1992) as a point, or points, in an individual's life which causes extreme and almost intolerable suffering to them, their friends and/or family. For the men in this study, rock bottom was often an existential moment, and quite simply meant a realisation that their addiction was unsustainable given the impact on their mental health, interpersonal relationships and physical wellbeing. Simply put their addiction and associated behaviours were killing them and damaging the identity and relationships which they valued. Rock bottom was also the point at which the men realised that they wanted to recover, to stay alive and move onto a new chapter in their lives. While some of the men in this study refer to a single incident as their *rock bottom*, others use the phrase to refer to a general period of time or an emotional low.

While rock bottom was the term used, we propose in this chapter that participants were on a *rocky road*, rather than hitting an objective moment or event that was a definitive rock bottom. That is, they often felt as if they had hit rock bottom, they would then engage in some intervention programme or attempt some life changes but unfortunately relapse and plummet to a new low, often a more destructive period than what went before. The journey out of addiction is a difficult one and relapse is common. Despite knowing this, relapse was seen as another failure by the men, and this often left them feeling spiritually and mentally broken. However, most men, once they had seen that there was a path out of addiction and relatedly crime, remained committed to repeatedly trying.

The participants spoke about looking towards another life—they had witnessed successes in their community, in the prison and in addiction support meetings. The local men who had succeeded in achieving recovery were very important role models for the participants as they battled addiction. Much like the importance of community role models in influencing their behaviour in a negative way in their youth, the new role models within their community, those who had succeeded in their recovery, were important pro-social models for the participants in this study.

This chapter shows, however, that it took significant courage, determination, perseverance and support to learn how to live a new life in recovery and leave their past life behind. This chapter is a testament to the hurdles our participants had to overcome. Positive support from peers, practitioners and particularly people in addiction support meetings helped the men construct new identities, reimage their past selves, and ultimately change their perception of what it means to be a man. Instead of prioritising a hegemonic masculinity, they learned that masculinity could be about being a father, a provider and a positive contributor to society. Their journey did not, however, end there. All the men reported the need to continue living a 'good life' to avoid slipping back down the road to addiction and crime.

The Rocky Road

All of the men in this study, when they reflected on their time in active addiction, pointed to the role of alcohol and drugs as a means of soothing past traumas, but also as a means of developing the protective hard-man image. Alcohol and drugs served a purpose, they were functional to a point, and often the men saw no other options. All the men in this study reported reaching a point whereby the alcohol and drug were not soothing the emotional pain of trauma, or facilitating socialisation, but was rather creating new traumas, damaging their mental and physical health, fracturing their relationships and damaging their own sense of self.

All of the participants used the language of *rock bottom* to describe the point at which they sought to act in an effort to deal with their lifestyle. While this is a retrospective analysis of their experiences and they frame the decision to act on their addiction as *a turning point* or a moment in time, the idea of rock bottom more broadly as being a motivator for behaviour change is supported in the research literature (Carlsson, 2012; Chen, 2018; Irving, 2016; Marsh, 2011; Redko et al., 2007; Sobell et al., 1996). Participants in a study by Marsh (2011: 60), for example, reported that their initial decision to enter a 12-step programme 'came from a sense of desperation engendered by mental and physical collapse'. Of course, these turning points are personal experiences, that is, we all have different ideas of what is painful and very different conceptions of rock bottom. Furthermore, rock bottom can be cumulative, it is seldom a one-off event but often a series of negative events. For some rock bottom was being constantly broke (P24), incapable of work (P17) or generally unable to function (P11) rather than a discrete moment in time.

A theme that emerged from the men's account of rock bottom was their sense of all-encompassing failure. Most reported that as they approached rock bottom, that no one wanted them around, they were isolated, lonely, unemployed, ill, weak and vulnerable.

> Because no one wanted to be around me, because I was just a mess. I was barred from the majority of bars in Cork city, I could not go out. My idea of going for a drink was up the park having a few cans. (P32)

Their ability to function, to meet their day-to-day needs, had become limited. This was a consequence of prioritising alcohol or drugs above other physical, emotional and social needs. This often brought poverty to their family, and chaos to the family home, if they were still living in a family home. Many identified the realisation that their addiction was harming their family as rock bottom, this theme repeatedly emerged as a low point in the men's lives. The inability to provide for their families, at Christmas for example, brought a sense of shame and self-loathing:

> I can remember very low points in my life, one of them was, I can remember Christmas 5 years ago, and I had nothing and I could not give my kids nothing for Christmas that was a hard one to take. Then I was telling myself, things were never this bad, how did I leave things get this bad. They were the hard parts. (P37)

While all participants experienced rock bottom in varying ways and with varying intensities, Paternoster and Bushway (2009) argue that it is the cumulative negative consequences of addiction and crime that ultimately become too taxing. It is this culmination of events which spurs the decision to change rather than one particular event.

> I was still on the streets, I was completely smashed, I was broken enough to want recovery, I was broken enough to be in a treatment house. No one wanted me around, I could not sleep in anyone's house. Lost friends, I was left with myself. And when no one wants you it is tough. I was picking drugs over my own child. (P33)

> I was sick of letting people down. I ended up homeless numerous times. It was a rocky road. (P37)

Many, like P37 and P25, reflected on feeling they had hit rock bottom multiple times. P25 would stop consuming drugs for a time, but then relapse, which was followed by a deepening of his addiction:

> I taught I hit rock bottom, and then I hit another one and it got worse. (P25)

P37 did not identify one rock bottom, his account was more like a rocky road descending down a mountain, with peaks and dips, twists and turns. Paternoster and Bushway's (2009) concept of the 'feared self' captures how the men felt in moments of clarity—they knew their options were death or recovery. They knew they had to choose:

> I would be dead, and that's the truth. (P15)

> I am delighted I caught it when I did because if I did not, there was worse things, I know that, heroin that was the next step for me. (P37)

The rocky road of addiction is not easy; sustaining addiction requires an almost singular focus on feeding a debilitating habit at the cost of everything else. The lifestyle led to the men being 'burnt out'. They had lost the drive and stamina needed to continue meaningfully functioning in their day-to-day lives. Ultimately, for the men, choosing sobriety, and relatedly choosing to stop offending or at least choosing to try, was a process of choosing peace of mind over chaos, but even more fundamentally, it was about choosing to survive in the first instance.

Identity Survival and Starting Anew

For the men in this study, maintaining their lifestyle and identity was physically and emotionally exhausting. The extreme nature of their drug and alcohol consumption, street fighting, aggression and risk-taking could lead only to prison or death; however, this chaos was the only lifestyle they ever knew. The level of dysfunction in the men's lives meant that in order to change, they needed to relearn almost every aspect of their day-to-day life, alter their sense of identity, their understanding of themselves and their interaction with others. This process made the men very vulnerable because the lifestyle the men followed was functional for them, it was a means of coping; a strategy learnt out of necessity. Their identity was intricately tied up with their behaviour and life choices, however, letting go of this identity was essential to recovery:

> They would be vulnerable, they are left on their own, that macho element comes away… I do not think I would survive, it's a survival skill, this is who I am do not take it away from me. (P9)

While recovery and desistance involved an identity shift, the reality was that the identities the men had cultivated had already started to fall apart because of their long-term excessive and problematic alcohol and/or drug consumption. The men did not initially want to let go of their hard-man image, but ultimately had little choice. They could no longer defend themselves, let alone be the aggressor, and they were no longer respected. Rather than hard men, they were seen as 'junkies' and addicts to be pitied or ridiculed (see Mullins, 2006). In short, the very behaviours that they prioritised as macho, the behaviours they inherited to survive on the streets became the very behaviours that led to their destruction:

> My identity was become more of a drunken fool than anything else. That womanizer, tough man that could earn a living was gone. (P30)

> I can remember getting into a fight and being knocked to the floor and everything, and you would be saying this should not be happening to me. (P8)

Losing their hard-fought image affected their mental well-being and left them in a very vulnerable place:

> What would that mean to have people think that you were not a good fighter? (Graham)

> My self-esteem would have been very low because of it, because I feel like, that's the area, that's the environment that I grow up in. (P21)

> I could not keep up the front anymore, I was bait [worn down] from the alcohol and the drugs at the time. (P16)

For the men in this study, the inability to live up to a particular interpretation of masculinity served as one of the catalysts for change. This was because they suffered existentially in terms of their sense of self and identity, but also because performing masculinity had a very narrow meaning in their community, and not being able to live up to this ideal led to ridicule, abuse and isolation. For some, this was part of reaching rock bottom.

Death or Recovery

In the sample for this study, relapse rates were very high—all the men experienced relapses, which often escalated the severity of their addiction (see Hser, 1997: 543), and impacted their mental and physical health. Twelve of the men attended a residential treatment centre more than once, and one attended a centre five times, but all of the men attempted recovery a number of times in various ways (i.e. outpatient treatment). All of the men attended AA and/or NA. One factor that influenced the likelihood of relapse was individual motivation to attend treatment. The men felt that coerced treatment, through court mandate, for example, was not conducive to recovery:

> I went to a treatment centre in 2005, I went for the wrong reasons, I went because I was after committing a crime, I got caught, I was after getting a book of evidence, I had two books, I said for 5 minutes of madness I am not going to go down for 5 years. I am going to go to treatment. But it was never going to work because I was going for the wrong reasons. I was in the treatment centre for 15 months. (P32)

P32 quickly relapsed but later willingly attended treatment.

> When you go in there [residential treatment centre] it was for myself, not for anyone else, I've had a great experience, I went in there no charges or anything. It gave me the key to go back into the meetings. (P36)

The men felt that those most likely to commit to treatment where the ones who had journeyed on a rocky road, reached what they thought was the end of the line, and could see no other option other than death.

Cycles of Relapse

Being open to engaging in treatment for addiction, and achieving recovery from addiction are of course two separate processes. While getting in the door is a major success, sticking at it and achieving sobriety is a lifelong process. Succeeding in recovery is linked to a complex array of factors but an important element is the narrative one tells oneself about addiction, choice, personal history and personal responsibility (Marsh, 2011). For the men, this is linked to psycho-education (knowing how and why we behave in certain ways) but also around narratives of blame and responsibility. For example, P40 reflected that he lacked understanding of why he used drugs and the psychological impact drugs had on him. This inability to understand the antecedents to his drug-taking behaviour and the consequences of this behaviour limited his ability to stop using, even though he believed that his addiction would eventually kill him:

> I have always a fear of being clean, for what reason I do not know. There is always something in me that I need something [drugs]. And I know I don't need something, but there is something in my head that says you need to take something to function better. I don't function better, it is stupid thinking, but for some reason I'm at it so long, if I don't make a change now, there is not too many ways this is going to end up for me. (P40)

Other participants reported a misplaced confidence in their own self-control including a belief that willpower was enough to battle what they saw as a bad habit. They tried substituting one substance for another, which inevitably resulted in repeated relapses. Several men shared that they came to the realisation that certain behaviours were not only unhelpful or distracting but gateways back to active addiction. These behaviours included substituting for less harmful drugs, being in certain places (e.g. a pub, a street corner) and other risk-taking behaviours such as gambling, offending, risky sex, etc. Identifying these gateways often took time, trial, error and reflection to link certain places, behaviours and people with the risk of relapse:

> I thought I could use successfully, or I thought it would be different this time, I would come out thinking I won't use tablets but I will have pints, but it does not work like that because I will end back at square one very quickly, I would end up on tablets... and then when it got bad I would go back to treatment, and when I come out of treatment I would say I will have a few joints and wont drink, but that was not enough for me. (P15)

Gateways back to addiction often emerged when the men felt physically and mentally better and had stopped consuming drugs/alcohol. Some underestimated the strength of their addiction and presumed they had control over their behaviours and could engage in *linked behaviours* without consequence. The linked behaviours differed from one individual to the next, but they were mostly related to places and people, and importantly anything related to maintaining the hard-man identity. The men spoke of gambling and returning to old friends and hangouts. While some quickly learnt that certain places, people, behaviours and substances were the gateway back into active addiction this realisation was slower for others:

> Then 2 or 3 weeks I was grand, back eating, I was thinking I was grand. I went into a bookies and won £300 and I went out and had a pint, and I was back getting powders and tablets again, I went home and they said we can't have you coming home like this anymore. (P40)

The return to active addiction was often followed by involvement in crime. One participant described it as a cascade that would increase in intensity as the addiction became more severe:

> [I was] back fighting and drink driving, back getting into car crashes, now things were getting worse, the fights were more frequent and violent. (P16)

The men spoke of how each relapse caused a further deterioration in their physical and mental health, and that the chaos in their lives worsened. This deterioration was for a number of reasons, including a reduction in family support, but also because going in and out of recovery is taxing and the men realised that they only had finite emotional energy. They soon realised that they were in danger of suicide or overdose if the cycle continued:

> My mental health can't take any more of the life I've lived, even if I was to go out using for a couple of days, or God forbid if I took a drink, I would not get 12 months out there drinking and drugging...I would end up dead in a couple of weeks. I know that, my body or my mind can't take another relapse or recovery like. (P17)

Many came to this realisation, often multiple times, but relapsed anyway. For all of the men, relapse made the addiction and associated behaviours more extreme, further harmed their mental and physical health and ensured their life became even more chaotic. This downward spiral caused the men to see only two ways out: attempt recovery again or attempt suicide. Both options were chosen by the men in this study at different times, and unfortunately, one man who had participated in this study completed suicide before achieving recovery.

The Difficult Transition from Prison to the Community

Why and how people recover from addiction is difficult to capture, and there are both personogenic and situational factors at play and these can combine in any number of ways to assist and impede success. In effect the recovery and desistance journeys are equifinal—there are many ways to get to the same end point—and it can be a different journey for every person. Despite this, there are commonalities amongst the men in this study that point to some key issues that were relevant for them as they sought recovery. A particular issue for the men in this study was the psychological burden of their past. Feelings of guilt, shame and anxiety were common as they attempted to address their addiction and offending and these emotions were often barriers to recovery. For many, drugs and alcohol were used to mask feelings of guilt and shame and, removing alcohol and drugs (and in many cases gambling) from the equation allowed these emotions to bubble to the surface. This meant, that to achieve recovery the men had to deal with these emotions and the pattern of behavioural responses to these emotions but without the crutch of alcohol and drugs.

In addition to the need to deal with the psychological issues underpinning their substance misuse and offending, they also had the additional barrier of their social context, especially the peer networks that sustained their addiction and offending lifestyle. Hanging onto the hard-man culture was a trigger for relapse as was the failure to knife off (Maruna, 2001) from the existing peer groups. It often took many years to recognise this pattern, mostly because the focus was on abstinence from substance use rather than a focus on the toxic social dynamics that underpin the role of drugs in certain communities.

For some, prison life presented an opportunity to experience a different way of living. The life they experienced on the streets was marked by exclusion from education and employment. For some, prison provided their first experience of having a job and being trusted to do that job, or their first opportunity to engage in education in a meaningful way. The sheltered and controlled environment also allowed them to experience another way of interacting with people and being a part of something positive:

> Just working in the kitchen, I was a trustee, the first time anybody ever trusted be in that setting. (P20)

Of course these experiences do not transfer automatically to life outside of prison and things often became chaotic again upon release. Back in the community, many experienced strong feelings of anxiety, fear and shame, feelings partly generated by relapsing and failing to maintain the plans set in prison, but also fear and shame about their past behaviour and how people viewed them. The men were often quick to self-medicate as a means of releasing the anxiety:

> I felt ashamed, I would have a thing in my stomach, now I would be delighted they were leaving me out, but when I was coming down Rathmore Road [Cork Prison] I would get desperate fear, I would have to drink. (P27)

Many participants were aware of the stigma attached to addiction and imprisonment (see Chen, 2010). This often resulted in increased feelings of shame and social isolation whilst in recovery. While in their early years, going to prison was a badge of honour, as they got older, they realised that they were being judged by their broader community and not just their peers. Being negatively labelled was also a barrier to recovery and desistance: McNeill (2016) speaks about tertiary desistance as the process of being accepted back into a community and how a lack of community acceptance can be a significant barrier for individuals trying to desist.

> I used to think I was ashamed of what I done, people saying in my neighbourhood he is only out of prison. (P27)

One participant became actively involved in the prison education unit and dedicated his time in prison to recovery from addiction. However, the shame he felt about past behaviour, coupled with the stress of returning to his community led to an almost immediate return to drinking and drug use on release, and eventually a swift return to active addiction. The transition was made more difficult by the lack of joined-up services. Men who had achieved sobriety in prison reported being housed in temporary accommodation in large dorms where drug use was rampant, so much so that some chose to sleep on the streets to avoid the temptation in the shelters. Others reported long waits for referrals to community addiction services, or having their addiction services disrupted; leading ultimately to relapse.

P12 similarly struggled to manage the transition from prison to community, partly because he had to deal with his past actions without drugs which had been his primary means of coping with difficult emotions:

> Getting out of prison, and having to face everybody with no drugs, the shit I was after leaving behind me, it was the hardest thing I had to come out and face. (P12)

Peer pressure was also an important part of the transition from prison to community and the pressure to return to the *old life* was often significant. The men spoke of being given money and drugs on release; drugs were even slid under one participant's front door. Many felt trapped by old associations, alliances and identities—they struggled to find a way out of their old life, and there were many things pulling them back.

> I had every plan, from the first time I went in there, I used to go to the Bridge Recovery group, to the educational unit, I used to be doing courses. I would ring my mother once a week and I would have the best intentions, I would be saying *never again*, but I could not help it. You come out the [prison] gate for about three hours and reality kicks in, society, I used to get paranoid again, and I used to get ashamed again, and I would end up going drinking. You would be celebrating as well, a fella would give you money, they would be drug dealing and they would give you a few pound for getting out. You are back doing the same thing. (P27)

Others talked about the temptation presented by simply meeting old acquaintances:

> I was around about a week, and some fellow asked my for a light, and then he asked me did I want some tablets, my first reaction was no, but when he left, I was [thinking] I should have taken them, it would have been nuts. Fellows I was in Simon [homeless accommodation] with would ask me to help them shoot up, in the street, because I would have been good at shooting up. And I would be there to them I am clean, and they would be saying so what, you are only injecting me, they could not get their heads around it. (P12)

The peer pressure, the expectation of old acquaintances, the old loyalties and the impact of hegemonic masculinity were overwhelming, these were very often triggers for the men and gateways back to addiction. Many felt judged by their peers because they had themselves often judged others who had attempted to abstain from drinking and drugs or desist from offending. Seeing others attempting to recover had a duel effect. It was, on the one hand, seen as a rejection of the peer group and their culture. On the other hand, those who succeeded in recovering became vital in motivating them to attempt recovery: they became positive role models:

> I was very anxious for the first couple of years, up around my own area, I taught people might look at me and say who does he think he is now, people would think that I was after getting snobby or posh. We used to think that anybody that has gone straight has gone posh, anyone that went to college from my area, my mentality was that anyone that went to college was rich people, posh people, and now to think that I am in UCC [the local university], and there is nothing abnormal about it for me - but my thinking around it before was mad. (P15)

This extract shows how 'going straight' (desisting and being in recovery) was seen as a cultural betrayal. Going straight dovetailed with being 'posh', which was an anathema to the working class foundation of Cork's Northside. This created a barrier to change because, not only were they losing the hard-man image, and their connection to their working-class roots, but they were actively seen as betraying their peers, their community and their culture. Many feared being ridiculed and alienated from the community they were so tied to in the past.

It was rare that the men had positive role models from their area. Few of their peers finished secondary school let alone attended third-level education. Education was seldom encouraged in the home and 'wasn't done' in these working-class communities:

> There was no one in my area that went to college, no one in recovery; it was just the way it was. (P25)

> It's not like other parts of the city where it is encouraged to go to college … people were going to prison. (P15)

Most of the men left school early, but many re-engaged with education whilst in prison. Attendance at prison education units was seldom initially motivated by a desire for learning, it was usually because the men wanted a distraction from the monotony of prison life or sought shelter from the drug and gang activity in the prison.

> [I] took all the classes to keep me away from the [prison] yard, away from the hassle, the drug taking the carry on. I did not want to fall in with that crowd at this stage. (P13)

The experience of education in the prison was often enough to provide a starting point for further education. For example, by engaging with the prison education unit, P31 realised that education was a means of making a living legally and moving away from his previous behaviours and identity. He started his education journey in prison but continued it upon release:

> I said I was going to get an education in prison, then I am going to do my trade, done that. Then I said I will do level 5 and 6 done that. Then 3rd level, in my second year, now thinking about doing a masters. I don't see why that won't happen, now I'm talking about plans after that. I made it well when I was a criminal, I made lots of money. I don't see why not I can't do it on the legit side ether. (P31)

P25 initially identified education as a means of accessing social welfare payments, he decided that he could learn how best to benefit from the social protection system if he was more educated. But the experience of learning exposed him to other options and ultimately he started studying at university:

> I applied for social studies and applied psychology in .... [pre-University institution], I got an interview and I got in, I went into it and I loved it. I applied for UCC [University] and I got that, and I am still in UCC now. (P25)

For some of the men, the services that enabled a continuity between prison and community support were especially important. These services are often provided by probation-funded projects and they start to work with the men while they are still in prison, helping to prepare for and support the transition to the community. P13 recalled how he immediately started drinking and gambling on his first night out of prison, however, knowing where the support was and who to reach out to prevent him from drifting back into active addiction:

> When I was talking with one of the staff from the Alliance [centre] I asked her what was there for me when I get out. I said to her when I get out I am going straight to the bookies, and what money is left I will go and get some drink, she said to call into the office when I get out. So I got ... two bottles of cider, went to the bookies and got drunk, next day I picked up the phone and said I am going back to the same way as before I went in. They told me to come straight in. From that day on I have not looked back, because I took full advantage of the services that they were giving me. (P13)

Maintaining Recovery: The Reality of Social Influence and Social Bonds

Researchers have suggested that the necessary life changes that support desistance from crime often involve removing oneself from engaging with certain people, and avoiding environments and situations which can lead them back to old behaviours, a process Maruna (2001; Maruna & Roy, 2007) calls 'knifing off'. Most participants realised the importance of this process for their recovery and desistance early on. This is not, however, an easy process (see Seaman & Lynch, 2022b).[1] The men in this study felt they had to knife off completely and in many cases even moved to live in another part of the city. They realised that rehabilitation within their community would be difficult and they needed to make a fresh start where people did not know of their past, and where opportunities to use and offend were lower:

> I don't think I would have stayed clean if I lived there. I would have went back to the same environment, back home, it would have been the same thing. (P19)

Not only did leaving their home area allow the men to avoid returning to their old lifestyle, merely by force of habit or opportunity, the anonymity

[1] While this book is primarily concerned with men, and there are particular issues for women or individuals with caring responsibilities—where walking away or knifing off, even temporarily, is often not a possibility (Seaman & Lynch, 2022b).

allowed them to dodge the stigma they carried within their own communities (see Ahmed et al., 2001) and avoid the ridicule associated with becoming *posh*. Some talked of wiping the slate clean:

> I was full of anxiety and fear the thought of going up there and be reminded of who I was, I am a different person now, I am not a junky or a scum bag anymore, I am living a clean and honest life. The people up there remember me as the old person, when they look at me the same way, I had that all going on in my head, so I thought I am not going to go near it, I am anonymous out in XXX [other part of the city], I am anonymous in the city. Nobody knows me, they only know me from who I am now, and I am happy for that at the moment. (P15)

> I stay away from the people I used to hang around with, I stay away from people who drink, stay away from pubs, stay away from hotels. (P36)

Knifing off was both geographical and social. The men reported how, if they bumped into old friends, they could only salute them and then had to walk away:

> I would just say hallo, and good bye, I would not even stop to talk to them. That's what I need to do to look after myself. (P36)

Knifing off was not, however, necessarily a permanent activity. Many described needing space to build resilience and, become stronger and more secure in their recovery and desistance journey. As time went by they became less vulnerable and better able to deal with peer pressure and people and memories from their past. Knifing off is not always about cutting the roots, but about the choice to walk away, and then actively choose who to allow back into your life. Some of the men in this study, however, felt that they could never engage fully with past friends and acquaintances, regardless of how strong and resilient they had become. This was a difficult realisation at first but became easier with time:

> It does not bother me as much as it used before. I can walk the other way so I do not have to bump into them. (P21)

All or Nothing: 'I changed my behaviours I changed everything'

A key theme that emerged in this study, one that accounts for all of the other sub-themes of recovery and desistance was the idea of living a good life. This idea of living a good life was portrayed by the men as the antithesis of their previous existence. As they described it, a good life was an honest life, being a good person, clean living, avoiding substance abuse and gateway behaviours and having sincere relationships. All participants felt that, for them, staying in recovery involved living this honest life, staying on this path, and importantly it was all or nothing, there were no half measures. The men pointed out that they either choose this good, honest life, or they risked their recovery and desistance. This involved fundamental changes to almost every part of their lifestyle, behaviour and identity, and so was often the most difficult element of recovery and desistance. For example, some initially felt they could address their addiction but still sell drugs, or avoid alcohol but hang around with old drinking buddies. These behaviours were often gateways back into more serious offending and active addiction. It often took many attempts at recovery, and many periods of incarceration, for the men to realise that they had to change all problematic behaviours if they wanted to maintain recovery. Life in recovery became easier once they realised and was accepted this.

> Everything changed, I suppose in the early days I was still selling drugs to buy a tracksuit, I kept on to some behaviours because I taught they were acceptable. I am clean off drugs and going to my meetings now, but I changed my behaviours, I changed everything. (P19)

After a few attempts at recovery P24 realised that minor offences and gateway behaviours had led to him relapse in the past:

> I've had been clean a few times before, one year, eighteen months, the difference this time is that everything has to change. When I was clean before, I could be selling tobacco, hanging around with the old mates, scamming the dole, illegal stuff, minor, but still illegal, it's still part of the system, it was like having my feet in both [worlds]. (P24)

Another significant hurdle was detaching themselves from the type of masculinity they had prioritised in the past. Certain behaviours associated with the form of masculinity prioritised in their peer group were not conducive to recovery (see also Dwyer, 2014). Recovery forced all participants to fundamentally reassess how they conceived of masculinity and what it meant to be a man:

> I am acting out left right and centre, with women, chasing women..... going to nightclubs and pubs pulling women. (P25)

> Even me chasing women and being involved with different women, I had to stop all that shit as well. (P24)

The men talked about living dishonestly, not necessarily committing a crime or abusing substances, but what they called the undercurrent or gateways to those behaviours. The men often pointed to the risk-taking element of their behaviour. They recognised the thrill-seeking involved in offending (Katz, 1988) and the high from drugs and alcohol, but it often took time to realise that they were seeking this high in other ways, not necessarily in illegal or harmful ways, but ways which put them on the path to more problematic behaviours. The men also spoke about how thrill-seeking behaviours were at odds with their new emerging identity.

> Its false, you would be talking in meetings saying how I am after changing my life and doing new things, then coming outside the door and fucking trying to make money of someone, or trying to ride this one, because her fella is away. It's the undercurrent stuff, the thrill kind of thing. (P24)

Participants also reflected on how dishonesty impacted their sense of self, self-worth and self-belief. Living honestly became vital because they identified achieving recovery and desistance as linked to living a good life and seeking peace of mind, which could be jeopardised by engaging in risky or gateway behaviours:

> I have to work on my conscience, my conscience must be clean for me to progress, and for my self-belief to come and my self-worth. And before when I was not working on that stuff I was going backwards. (P24)

> I was on the brink of taking drugs most days. When I started changing that behaviour, things started to get easier, like the emotional stuff. (P19)

Social Bonds and Role Models

Early recovery was the time period seen as most challenging by the men in this project; they felt vulnerable, lonely and isolated during this time. Most identified the importance of building new (positive and pro-social) support networks (see McNeill, 2006; Laub & Sampson, 2003), and becoming part of pro-social groups with shared aims and values. This supported the development of a new social identity whilst in early recovery (Tajfel, 1978). The measures needed to support recovery and desistance namely, identity, a new peer group and support networks are all prioritised by addiction support organizations such as NA and AA and all of the men in this study, at one time or another, engaged with these organisations.

The importance of role models was highly significant for individuals in this research. Importantly, however, role models had to be relatable and accessible—the participants also spoke about *insider* role models, individuals with the same background and the same identity experiences as themselves. Men who had similar life experiences as themselves, and had achieved recovery were a source of great hope—these were the role models the men wanted and needed. Ironically, the role models the men ultimately looked up to were often men who they had previously used drugs with, drank with, or been incarcerated with. This of course made them and their achievements seem more realistic and attainable, but most importantly, the men and their role models once again had the same aims, although this time they were positive and ultimately pro-social aims: recovery, desistance and living a good life.

Seeing the transformation achieved by individuals who attended 12-Step type meetings (or other treatment programs) provided the participants in this study with motivation to engage with the process of recovery for themselves. These long-term AA/NA members often offered to sponsor some of the men in this study; they showed them how they were living their lives without alcohol and drugs, and the changes needed to maintain recovery. Also important in this process was the sense of belonging to a new social group, a new social identity that was relevant to their current place in life, and also finding friendships to alleviate the loneliness and isolation. The creation of this new in-group made it easier to create distance between participants and their former friends and family. It made knifing off easier because there was a new social network ready for them to become part of.

Finally, by having a new identity reference, they were more clearly able to identify who they no longer were and who they could become. While Laub and Sampson (2003) identify the importance of social bonds for deterring offending, these bonds also play an additional role in providing the basis for forming a new identity and the shedding of the old:

> Everybody says it [AA/NA] is not a social club, but for me it is. That attachment thing, the bonding thing, that feeling of being a part of something again you know. And again that thing of off-loading and people understanding of where you are at, and where you're trying to go, now that thing, birds of a feather flock together, I gravitated to the people I taught were doing well. (P12)

P36 found it helpful to see how other members of 12-Step Meetings had similar experiences but were able to progress in life and, had not returned to addiction:

> They were just as bad as myself, if not worse, I thought I was the only person. They're off the drink years, they have their family back, they are living the life of Reilly, they did not have to go back to the person there were. (P36)

The men regarded the meetings as peaceful spaces which offered time for reflection and isolation from daily stresses:

> I go to my meetings and it might be for a hour a day, I describe it as being naked, I have no distractions, no TV, phone, nothing to distract me, and that's where I know where I am at. (P25)

At these meetings, some of the men re-established old friendships, and this eased the transition into their new life. McNeill (2006) highlights the importance of developing a trusting relationship with people who can help support transitions out of crime and addiction, but the pain and suffering brought about by *knifing off* cannot be underestimated; having the option to keep some positive relationships from their past whilst going through recovery was welcomed:

> I went to an NA meeting, and I met a fella I knew and he was going to the meeting, then a car pulled up with three of my friends, they got out and they were going to the meeting, that's how it all started....It started me on this track that I am still on. I was only two days out. (P26)

P16 also met an old friend at a meeting. Seeing the change he had made motivated him to continue with the process:

> I went to the AA meeting and the funny thing was a lad that I used to hang around with that was after disappearing, I did not know what happened to him, he was a state, he was a mess, and there he was looking all fresh in the meeting, he was telling me he was doing Thai boxing. (P16)

Existing research shows that an AA/NA affiliation can provide a sense of belonging for people trying to recover from substance abuse and this can increase an individual's sense of overall general social support and belonging which helps abstinence-specific self-efficacy (Stevens et al., 2015).

There is also an important overlap in how AA/NA support can assist in desistance work: many of the men had used violence in the past, they had been violent within a subculture which demanded violent responses to confrontation. Managing their violence and aggression became an essential element in their journey. Learning alternatives to violence, how to avoid violence and communicate without violence, were key elements of both recovery and desistance. Part of the AA/NA journey is learning about recognising and communicating needs, and this has relevance for conflict resolutions and strategies for dealing with confrontation. This had implications for the men in how they managed existing relationships and controlled their own reactions to stress and conflict more generally.

> I started to learn that I could not shout and roar, I could not be angry; I could not be losing my temper. I just went to meetings, and I got honest with myself and others. (P39)

> You learn that you do not have to act with violence, you can talk or express your anger through words or talk instead of digging someone in the head. (P15)

The people P15 met at 12-Step meetings showed him that violent behaviour was not normal and he eventually learned alternative ways to interact with people. That is, the meetings challenged the basis of the hard-man identity common amongst the participants. Ultimately this meant the men had to unlearn the Street Code by challenging their established definitions of, and ideas about, respect and disrespect, masculinity and what it was to be a man. They had to learn to walk away from conflict rather than react to all perceived slights or instances of perceived disrespect:

> If someone disagree with yah, or someone insults you …you must confront them straight away, and that's the way it is, but when you come into recovery you learn that that is actual madness. (P15)

> I was challenged on everything up there, all my behaviours, I was challenged on it and I needed it because they were off the wall. Aggression, violence, not fighting but violent conduct, being aggressive towards someone, and coming into conflict all the time. When I came out of there then, say if someone today is disrespecting towards me, I would be very comfortable handling it vocally, or I would not get worked up. (P15)

Crime, lifestyle and alcohol/drug use were intertwined for the men. For example, some participants were tempted back to crime after being in recovery for extended periods of time. This was often because they were accustomed to earning money through crime, and had few alternative means of making money.[2] Committing crimes was, however, almost always a gateway back to active addiction:

> That thinking that I could go back selling drugs, and stay clean, but again for myself, that thought pattern comes in I have to look at myself, I could be insecure about myself, fix it with money. Or if I am lonely, the thing of being wanted. (P12)

Others reported missing the excitement of their past lifestyle. For example, P21 reported being 'addicted to the lifestyle'.

[2] Many of the men reported that keeping busy helped in their rehabilitation. While this included paid employment, many of the men were unprepared for the workforce, lacking social and cultural skills needed to maintain a job. Instead, meaningful activity was the first step. Studying, personal development courses and volunteering often helped the men learn how to be stable, achieve peace of mind and slow down.

> It was such a big part of my life, I struggle living normal... I miss the adventure. It used to be every weekend, every single day there was an argument, some sort of crime thing. I was addicted to the lifestyle more than anything. (P21)

A key issue for the men was to identify the linkages between their needs and their behaviours and how they thought about meeting these needs. For those seeking thrills, the processes underpinning the need for excitement and how to deal with this needed to be a part of their recovery journey; for those seeking approval and acknowledgement from risk-taking behaviour, getting to the root of that need was essential. Not everyone was on the same journey, but they were all trying to find a way to identify and manage the issues that led to addiction in the first place.

Resisting the Pull of Family, Friends and Violence

Addiction does not happen in isolation, nor does recovery, and the dynamics of interpersonal and inter-familial relationships are a key part of the process. Oftentimes family and friends were a risk to recovery; they sought to pull the person back into problematic relationships and the men knew they had to actively *resist* this. For the men in this study, the initial motivation to knife off could weaken and, depending on the intensity of the relationship dynamics, contact might recommence just as the recovery process progressed. Peers in rehabilitation, treatment providers and support workers all warned participants of the dangers of becoming involved in the feuds and dramas involving family and friends and how this was a risk to recovery, but the pressure was often intense. For example, P19 was convinced to become involved in an escalating violent conflict after telephoning a friend whose house had been attacked:

> I rang a fellow to see how he was getting on, because I heard his aunt's house was after getting petrol bombed, and straight away he wanted me to go on, we will have you back by 10 o clock, I was saying I can't, they still had a hold over me, I was saying I can't I am in treatment, I was saying that I can't with my court case. (P19)

When P30's brother was assaulted as part of an ongoing feud, the pressure to become involved, coming from his family, almost pushed him back to drinking:

> My brother was hit. The panic and the fear on how do I stay sober and try and not get involved in it. The guards came, I nearly took a drink, I was 12 months sober... I was tormented. (P30)

At the core of feuding is the status and prestige of the family (not just the individual), the need to be seen as a man by defending the family. Responding to threats to the family was prioritised as a key function of a *hard-man,* this was due to the need to preserve the individual's status, but also to avoid being seen to be disrespected, and worse still tolerating this disrespect (Hourigan, 2011; Hourigan et al., 2018; Windle, 2019). This made it very difficult for the men to reject requests to support their family, even when it was a direct threat to their recovery and desistance. A failure to get involved would be seen as a betrayal and could result in being ostracised from family and friends, while also opening oneself up to being victimized.

> I can remember lads that did step away and did not want anything to do with it, there were being called rats, sneaks, there were getting beatings, I would just fall in calling them rats. (P19)

Feuding was a key part of the performance of masculinity, and this seriously interfered with the recovery journey. Resisting pressure from family and friends to get involved in disputes and feuds was a difficult and often ongoing battle—some knew that becoming involved in feuding would trigger other linked behaviours, and they would ultimately return to active addiction. Not becoming involved was also risky though, for it ignited the old feelings about being seen as weak which still haunted the men.

> I can manage the drugs by myself but it's the other thing [involvement in a family feud] which is the problem ... I can be pulled into that kind of life... it's been such a big part of my life, it is tough. (P34)

Some did, however, disengage from the feuds. For example P8 was adamant that he would break the intergenerational tradition of family feuding and, like many of the men who discussed feuds, he was concerned for his children:

> You have the next generation now growing up, and they are attacking my niece, my niece is a quiet girl. It's like what my brother is doing is having a ripple effect on my niece. So hopefully break the cycle with my kids. My kids are not going to be going out doing that; they are not going to look up to that. (P8)

In short, the men were aware that engaging in violence was a trigger back to addiction, but disengaging from feuding was difficult. It was not just about making money or thrills, but rather the status of the family. The feuds were bigger than the individual and often inherited from parents. This made feuding a difficult gateway to avoid. It also meant that disengaging led to a lonely existence, because the men had to avoid family and friends, their home and community, at least in the short to medium term. This made the support networks of NA and AA and other organisations vital in providing the men with a meaningful chance at recovery.

Recovery, Identity Shift and the Public Self

Hegemonic masculinity (Connell & Messerschmidt, 2005) was a dominant force in the lives of all the participants in this study. Many of the men's sense of identity was intimately linked to performing a certain type of masculinity, specifically the use of violence, displays of aggression and achieving dominance over others. This performance was important at a cultural and community level and failing to perform in an expected way would lead to severe consequences, both in terms of sense of self, place in the community, and also physical safety. Beyond the current manifestations of masculinity and the interpretation of what it means to be a man for the individuals in this study, they spoke of the transgenerational transmission of these ideas and how they learnt this form of masculinity from their family and older generations on the streets. As far as the men were concerned, there was only one way to be a man, and respect could only be gained by adhering to this strict interpretation of masculinity.

While in recovery, participants identified their interpretation of masculinity as a barrier to sobriety and desistance. This was because their sense of being a man was not conducive to introspection, change or acceptance. It was also because they knew of nothing else, and had no other identity experience to draw upon with which to bring about change. Rehabilitation and desistance involved ultimately reconfiguring what it meant to be a man (Bendelow & Williams, 2005; Dwyer, 2014). This meant the men had very serious foundational psychological work to do in order to achieve personal change and ultimately recovery. Some found the start of the process particularly challenging, partly because they had to give up the identity and lifestyle they had strived for as children, one that was accepted and valued within their community. They had to learn a whole new way of living:

> My mind is stuck in limbo, I am very depressed, it's like I failed at that, it's like you are being born again. (P34)

> What did you fail at? (Graham)

> It's not that I failed, your ideas of the whole way you grow up, is wrong, now you have to be reborn into this other life. You know nothing really about it, it's like you are 30 years of age, and it's like where the fuck are you kind of thing. (P34)

Being seen as a tough man bolstered many participants' self-esteem. It was not until the men tried to pull away from this behaviour that they realised how much they valued this identity:

> I did not realize how much I liked it the bravado thing till I came out of it. (P9)

And how difficult it was to let go:

> I still have that persona around me, still have the loud mouth, fuck this fella, I don't give a fuck about that fella. Still had that attitude, or talk. I still would have the macho talk without the drink ... it was everything it was survival; it was the most important thing in my life. It was hard to let it go. It was hard to understand to let it go. (P39)

Others reported a need to maintain an aspect of the hard-man image to avoid being disrespected and victimised in the future. It's difficult to let go of behaviours designed to aid survival in a tough environment:

> It's gone to an extent in that I am not out there throwing my weight around. But I would like to think I can keep onto some bit for some day that I might need it, when someone tries' it on with me again. I would

> like to think it is there to mind me. But not for any reason for me to do anything, not to make myself look bigger, for any bad reason. (P31)

> These things have kept bullies and people who wanted to get at me at bay, they kept me alive, I would be afraid to let it go, if I let it go someone might harm me, like the way I was when I was a child. (P31)

All eventually felt a need to let go of the hard-man image altogether because it impeded effective communication and, often ended in violence and negative emotions, all of which were gateways back into active addiction:

> Going back to old ways going around with old people.... it is the way they be talking the lingo, it will take you right back there like, using again. (P8)

Being in recovery is all about change, and the extent of change needed is often underestimated. While most of the men acknowledged the need to change their identity and avoid old behaviours, this realisation often took many years and several relapses. For example, P8 had been in recovery for several years and distanced himself from his previous lifestyle, however, when a family member was attacked, he had a battle with himself. He was worried that others would view him as weak if he did not retaliate, even after all his years in recovery.

Getting to the point where an individual can detach themselves from performing this type of masculinity is a long and difficult journey. It left a void, and participants identified a sense of loss. They mourned the loss of a self that they valued, and that they know was valued in their community—they spoke of feeling worthless:

> You would not feel anything; you would not feel man enough. All that left straight away, all that was gone out of me. I felt worthless. (P26)

Others experienced a sense of relief at being able to distance themselves from their hard-man selves. They felt relief at no longer having to maintain a front and recognised the toxic impact of that identity performance on their well-being:

> I think it was easy for me to let go of that hard-man image because it was all a front, I was never really a violent person. (P32)

> And I know I will suffer from it. If I harm anyone I am the one who suffers mentally and emotionally I suffer from it. (P39)

The letting go of the hard-man identity had another positive impact on the process of recovery and desistance. It allowed the men to externalise the cause of their behaviour to a culture and an identity that meant they were not bad people but in a bad situation. It allowed them to construct what Maruna (2001) calls a redemptive narrative that pointed to an external force as being the source of, or influencing, past behaviours. That is not to say they don't recognise their own responsibility for their actions, but that they can move forward with the narrative that they are no longer in that *bad* situation and can be their true self free of negative influences. This detachment allows them to construct a new identity or more accurately expose their *real* identity as a predominantly *good person*:

> It was all a front, it was not the true me. That macho, the way I spoke, the way acted, the way I portrayed myself, the way I walk was a phony person, it was fake. (P39)

A reliance on redemptive scripts is a key part of successful desistance, and in research conducted with individuals who successfully desist from offending, the ability to distance oneself from past behaviours by contextualising that behaviour is indicative of the liklihood of achieving desistance (Maruna, 2001).

Role Models and New Identities

The participants in this study did not grow up with many, or sometimes any, positive male role models. They aspired to be like those men around them, tough, willing to use violence and respected; they aspired to be hard men. For many of the men, recovery was the first time they encountered what could be called positive male role models, people who could model a new alternative form of masculinity. Having a new way to be a man based on new values that aligned with seeking to live a good life was a revelation for many of the participants and one they uniformly embraced. Their conception of masculinity started to slowly shift away from a fixed identity based on what they learnt growing up to a more positive pro-social identity. When asked what being a man means to them today, the majority of the participants focused on the centrality of the family and giving back to society:

> Someone who gets up in the morning, goes to work and earns a living for himself, through honest means, I know now that the hardest thing in the world to do is to live honest, life is hard, and if you can get up in the morning and go about your day and not cause any harm to no-one, provide for your girlfriend or your wife, your kids, that is what a real man does. (P15)

Parenthood motivated many of the men to change. Becoming a father provoked them to consider their ideas about what it meant to be a man. This was their 'hook for change' (Giordano et al., 2002), but the reality of parenthood often made it very difficult for the men to achieve change.

> It's not just me anymore, I am a Dad now. (P34)

> If I did not have the child I would not be here. I would be dead or in prison. Having the child was a massive change. (P33)

Sampson and Laub (1993) suggest that crime is most likely to occur when social bonds are weakened or dissolved, however, this should be qualified by referring to pro-social bonds. For the men in this study, were well connected to their community and had tight networks of peers in their lives—this however antagonised their criminal involvement. The reality for the men in this study was that the creation of new pro-social bonds and meaningful relationships was key to their recovery and desistance, and the dissolution of existing bonds was beneficial for them because it allowed them to knife off from the toxic relationships that tied them to addiction and offending. For many of the men, abstinence from crime and substances had to come before meaningful positive relationships were possible.

Maturity and the Journey Through Recovery

The men in this study questioned the impact that substance abuse from a young age had on their emotional and cognitive development. P37 felt that drinking and taking drugs 'stopped him from maturing' and that it was not until he entered recovery that he started to learn how to experience the maturity that is expected of an adult. That is, while in recovery, he felt that he went back to the age he first started his addiction and began to mature from there. The evidence for this idea of re-experiencing development is varied, but psychoanalytic approaches support this interpretation of the freezing of development. According to Mortazavi and Arjmandi (2012) a thirty-year-old person who was dependent on drugs may perform like an adolescent in terms of emotional functioning because they effectively skipped aspect of their development by being catapulted from childhood to the adult hood without any transition period. This *freezing* of development can also be related to experiences of trauma. Recent neurological studies show that substance abuse during the teenage years can impair performance on memory tasks, attention, spatial skills and executive functioning (Squeglia et al., 2009).

> Since I came into recovery I am after being through a lot. I can remember I used to be smart in school, when I started drink and drugs it felt like I did not progress as an adult, I stopped at that age. And then when I got clean I had to learn, its like being born again, I had to learn how to deal with life. I went back to the age where I picked up [drugs]. (P37)

Many participants identified maturity as a factor in their success and also fatigue with the life they had been leading. Some identified being too young to attempt recovery or desistance:

> I know this way of life was for me it was something I was looking for. There was nun's priest, doctors everyone used to be making phone calls for me; I could not carry it out. Deep down I did not want to get clean and sober, at that time anyway, I was only young. (P27)

Others discussed slowly maturing out. That they reached a point whereby they were tired of living what they identified as an immature lifestyle:

> I think I was a lot more mature, I was very juvenile those years in prison, very immature, this time I went in I was like a family man, I was grown up, I was looking at young fellows now in their 20s talking all the shit they were talking about, and I was [thinking] that is not me anymore. (P17)

P13 also identified that being imprisoned at an older age forced a period of reflection. He had experienced multiple attempts at recovery and relapses, multiple stays in prison and substantial therapeutic interventions. None had worked, but all had helped him mature:

> At 40, I know I was getting too old for that carry on. I took a good luck at myself while I was in there for the three months; I was able to analyse myself and my life, where it is at and where it was going. (P13)

It also took time for the men to be willing to shift their perception of masculinity; they had to mature out of the hard-man image. Spector-Mersel (2006: 70) points to the influence of age on how we think about masculinities by suggesting that different ways of doing masculinity are 'bound to social clocks that ascribe different models of manhood to different periods in men's lives'. For some in this study, it took a few years in recovery for them to shift their idea of what it was to be a man:

> What age where you when you stopped looking up to the men that were in trouble? (Graham)

> After prison, 23 24, I am 26 now. (P21)

> 26 I was in treatment; I would have had clean time behind me. I got a bit mature in treatment. (P27)

P30 was in recovery for four years before his conception of masculinity shifted. He was 22 when he first went into recovery.

> About a year or two into sobriety, I kept all that negative stuff with me, I did not want to push that away yet. I still taught that was a part of my image you know. I found that very hard to push that away, it took about 2 or 3 years in sobriety, I left that behind you know. (P8)

A New Identity and Talking It Out

For the men in this study, the process of engaging in recovery work was difficult, because it was at odds with some of the values and behaviours that were so central to their way of life. For example, some participants, whether in counselling or group sessions, initially found it difficult to talk about their feelings, or in many cases even recognise their feelings. They learned at a very young age that showing certain emotions was a sign of weakness, and if you show weakness people will take advantage of you. Instead of talking about their emotions, the men had long relied on drink, drugs and violence as a means of expression or suppression. Furthermore, self-sufficiency is a core element of hegemonic masculinity, which makes it difficult to ask for help. Some attempted rehabilitation alone, totally isolated from their past but with no connections to a potential future, and this left them exceptionally isolated.

> I had to give up this idea that I could be self-sufficient, because it leads to loneliness, I developed a will to live which I lost. (P16)

Shapland and Bottoms (2011) suggest that isolation as a means to achieve desistance can limit and disadvantage the would-be desisters lives, which limits the chances of successful desistance and recovery. In a similar way, recovery is not all about the individual, it is about the individual in their community and so, while isolation may assist abstinence, it limits opportunities for relationship building, friendship and identity change. Learning to live a meaningful pro-social life is a key part of desistance and recovery, so isolation flies in the face of this aim. Several participants noted that, when they tried to go it alone, their mental health worsened and they used drinks or drugs to self-medicate.

All participants eventually learned the therapeutic benefits of talking and all eventually engaged in some form of talking therapy.

> If I can get over this thing about expressing my feelings to someone, and then I'll go from there, and I did, I was able to talk about what was going on inside my head, the tightness in my chest was going, so I felt I want more of that, I need more of it, and 4 years on down the line I am doing well, but I did literally pull myself out of the gutter, as I said I did not care if I lived or died. (P13)

Engaging in therapy alongside attending groups like AA or NA was essential for the men in this study. Seventy-two percent of them spoke about the adverse childhood experiences that were a part of their life growing up. It took a long time in therapy to make the links between childhood trauma, drug use, relationship problems, identity issues and recovery. Identifying why they behaved the way they did, understanding patterns in their behaviour and reconciling their past with the person they want to become is a lifelong journey for the men.

> The abuse I suffered at home from my mother that really affected me in a sense that I really lost compassion for human beings. I only know all this now, because I am learning in the last couple of years. I am in therapy for the last 5 years. (P31)

Finding Peace of Mind, Helping Others and Living a Good Life

In the later stages of recovery, many participants in this study began to look to the future. The literature on desistance often focuses inordinately on employment, but this is often not a realistic expectation for the men who have been in and out of prison, are suffering the effects of drug abuse and are still in the early years of recovery. The men in this study were unskilled, had chequered employment histories, or had never worked, and had criminal records. Anyone one of these factors is a problem for a job seeker. The options available to the men were limited, and the options for *meaningful* employment even more so. However, perhaps because of this, or in spite of this, the men focused on how they could give back by helping others deal with their own addictions. They saw their strengths as having achieved recovery and desistance and as such sought to use this experience to help others. Like Maruna's (2001) 'wounded healers', they wanted to give something back and express their gratitude for those who helped them. This helping took many forms, from enrolling in university programmes on youth work or counselling to acting as sponsor of 12-Step programmes to more casually helping friends and family members access recovery. Helping others signalled to themselves and others that they were good people, improved their self-esteem and helped shift their internal view of themselves (see Marsh, 2011). Helping others helped them to change their identity from people who took from or harmed society to people who gave back to society.

Many of the men shared what they were doing now, normal things which gave them a great deal of pleasure and pride. The basics of working and spending time with family were especially valued.

> Work, college, job, baby on the way, happy with my partner, family are progressing, I see them changing, things are good now. (P24)

> I never had a job interview, but I am after having two interviews in the last couple of weeks. One of them I might be getting, I am trying to build a structure, I am in the middle of getting an education, looking for work, looking for an apartment, set up a whole structure, meets my child a couple of nights a week. College 3 nights work two days. (P33)

I'm working, I get on well with my colleagues, I'm starting to recover physically, I have great relationships with my family and building relationships with my kids.

P25 reported losing all confidence in himself while in addiction, but three years into recovery:

Life has been good in general, I accomplished more in the last three years than I did in my whole life. I went to college, Fetac level 5 ... I got a distinction. I got a car I started driving I was off the road for drunk driving. I am back working, I play sport, I always had the interest in boxing, but never had the confidence to do it because I was fucked. I've had three boxing fights, and I have an MMA fight coming up. I am after doing loads of stuff for charity, marathons, bungee jumps, Ocean to City races, life has just progressed tenfold. (P25)

For P26 shedding his tough man image allowed him to find love:

The place I have been, I am after being on a plane 16 times the last two years, going to lovely places, I'm getting married, I would never think of these things, married what the fuck would I want to get married for. I wanted to be single, and going on with a different girl every few weeks. It might be nice to look at another woman, buts it is not for me. I am after finding the right person. (P26)

P32 discussed how recovery gave him the strength and resources to deal with challenges, and he was rightly proud of being there for his mother when she was sick:

My mother was diagnosed with cancer, I suppose with the help of a power greater than myself members, sponsors and general counsellors, I got through the last 12 months, recovery has giving me the ability to be there for my mother, and give back to her. I do believe I was meant to be clean for this time of my life, because if I was not I would be more worried what was going to happen to me, or what will happen to me, I do not believe I would get through it if I was using, it was the most testing time, I had to do a lot of work on myself, personal development, counselling, attending meetings, I done a lot of work on myself and it is standing to me today, to go through what I am going through and not wanting to use. (P32)

Some participants achieved their ultimate goal—peace of mind:

> .....the aim was to have some peace of mind. (P17)

> ......I just want a bit of peace and happiness. (P10)

References

Ahmed, E., Harris, N., Braithwaite, J., & Braithwaite, V. (2001). *Shame management through reintegration*. Cambridge University Press.

Bendelow, G., & Williams, S. J. (2005). *Emotions in social life: Critical themes and contemporary issues*. Routledge.

Carlsson, C. (2012). Using 'turning points' to understand processes of change in offending: Notes from a Swedish study on life courses and crime. *The British Journal of Criminology, 52*(1), 1–16.

Chen, G. (2010). The meaning of suffering in drug addiction and recovery from the perspective of existentialism, Buddhism and the 12-step program. *Journal of Psychoactive Drugs, 42*(3), 363–375.

Chen, G. (2018). Building recovery capital: The role of hitting bottom in desistance and recovery from substance abuse and crime. *Journal of Psychoactive Drugs,* (5), 420–419.

Connell, R. W., & Messerschmidt, J. W. (2005). Hegemonic masculinity: Rethinking the concept. *Gender and Society, 19*(6), 829–859.

DuPont, R. L., & McGovern, J. P. (1992). Suffering in addiction: Alcoholism and drug dependence. In P. L. Starck & J. P. McGovern (Eds.), *The hidden dimension of illness: Human suffering* (pp. 155–201). National League for Nursing Press.

Dwyer, D. (2014). The lived experiences of men in 12-step recovery against a backdrop of hegemonic masculinity. *Irish Probation Journal, 11*(1), 177–195.

Giordano, P. C., Cernkovich, S. A., & Rudolph, J. L. (2002). Gender, crime, and desistance: Toward a theory of cognitive transformation. *American Journal of Sociology, 107*(2), 990–164.

Hourigan, N. (2011). *Understanding Limerick*. Cork University Press.

Hourigan, N., Morrison, J. F., Windle, J., & Silke, A. (2018). Crime in Ireland north and south: Feuding gangs and profiteering paramilitaries. *Trends in Organized Crime, 21*(2), 126–146.

Hser, Y. I. (1997). Drug treatment careers: A conceptual framework and existing research findings. *Journal of Substance Abuse Treatment, 14*(6), 543–558.

Irving, J. (2016). Alcoholics anonymous: Sustaining behavioural change. In A. Robinson & P. Hamilton (Eds.). *Moving on from crime and substance use: Transforming identities*. Policy.

Katz, J. (1988). *Seductions of crime*. Basic Books.
Laub, J. H., & Sampson, R. J. (2003). *Shared beginnings, divergent lives: Delinquent boys to age 70*. Harvard University Press.
Marsh, B. (2011). Narrating desistance: Identity change and the 12-step script. *Irish Probation Journal, 8*(1), 49–68.
Maruna, S. (2001). *Making good: How ex-convicts reform and rebuild their lives*. American Psychological Association Press.
Maruna, S., & Roy, K. (2007). Amputation or reconstruction? Notes on 'knifing off' and desistance from crime. *Journal of Contemporary Criminal Justice, 23*(1), 104–124.
McNeill, F. (2006). Community supervision: Context and relationships matter. In B. Goldson & J. Muncie (Eds.), *Youth crime and justice* (pp. 125–139). Sage.
McNeill, F. (2016). Desistance and criminal justice in Scotland. In H. Croall, G. Mooney, & R. Munro (Eds.), *Crime, justice and society in Scotland* (pp. 200–216). Routledge.
Mortazavi, Z., & Arjmandi, A. B. (2012). Comparing attachment styles in opum addicts and non addicts. *European Journal of Experimental Biology, 2*(4), 927–930.
Mullins, C.W. (2006). *Holding your square: Masculinities, streetlife and violence*. Willan.
Paternoster, R., & Bushway, S. (2009). Desistance and the "feared self": Toward an identity theory of criminal desistance. *The Journal of Criminal Law and Criminology, 99*(3), 1103–1156.
Redko, C., Carlson, R. G., & Rapp, R. C. (2007). A folk model of treatment readiness among drug users in Ohio. *Journal of Ethnicity in Substance Abuse, 6*(2), 15–40.
Sampson, R., & Laub, J. (1993). Crime and deviance in the life course. *Annual Review of Sociology, 18*(1), 63–84.
Seaman, V. and Lynch, O. (2022a). Knifing off? Social networks and the inadequacies of desistance frameworks for women in the criminal justice system in Ireland. In Grace, S., O'Neill, M., Walker, T., King, H., Baldwin, L., Jobe, A., Lynch, O., Measham, F., O'Brien, K., & Seaman, V. (Eds.). *Criminal women; Gender matters* (pp. 20–35). Policy.
Seaman, V. and Lynch, O. (2022b). Perpetrators and victims: Women, double deviance, and the criminal justice system. In I. Masson & N. Booth (Eds). *Handbook of women's experiences in criminal justice*. Routledge.
Shapland, J., & Bottoms, A. (2011). Reflections on social values, offending and desistance among young adult recidivists. *Punishment and Society, 13*(3), 256–282.

Sobell, L., Cunningham, J., & Sobell, M. (1996). Recovery from alcohol problems with and without treatment: Prevalence in two population surveys. *American Journal of Public Health, 86*(7), 966–972.

Spector-Mersel, G. (2006). Never-aging stories: Western hegemonic masculinity scripts. *Journal of Gender Studies, 15*(1), 67–82.

Squeglia, L. M., Jacobus, J., & Tapert, S. F. (2009). The influence of substance use on adolescent brain development. *Journal of Clinical EEG and Neuroscience, 40*(1), 31–38.

Stevens, E., Jason, L. A., Ram, D., & Light, J. (2015). Investigating social support and network relationships in substance use disorder recovery. *Substance Abuse, 36*(4), 396–399.

Tajfel, H. E. (1978). *Differentiation between social groups: Studies in the social psychology of intergroup relations*. Academic Press.

Windle, J. (2019). The causes and consequences of gangland violence in the Republic of Ireland. In R. Lombardo (Ed.). *Organized crime: Causes and consequences* (pp. 110–123). Nova Science.

CHAPTER 8

Conclusion

Abstract This chapter presents a critique and overview of the findings from the Ground Theory analysis documented earlier. This study challenges some of the dominant assumptions associated with desistance in the criminological literature. It has raised the possibility that, in the case of addiction, desistance emerges as a side effect of recovery, not as an independent process. In addition, the life stories of the men in this study point to the importance of historically and culturally transmitted manifestations of masculinity in shaping the behaviour choices that ultimately lead to active addiction. Consequently, the data suggests that we must address issues of hegemonic masculinity, calling out cultures that prioritise violence, risk taking and bravado. We must challenge identities that are intimately linked to the kinds of masculinity prioritised in adolescence—these are all issues that are fundamental to achieving recovery and desistance. Challenging these identities requires more than words—these identities are founded on economic deprivation and social exclusion, and passed down across generations. Longer-term policies must focus on reducing inequalities. Furthermore, in the words of one of the men, in order to recover and desist you have to live an *honest life*. Not doing crime and not consuming drugs or alcohol, is not success. For the men in this study, being kind, thoughtful and introspective and contributing to society were how they judged success. The path to success was about honesty, avoiding problematic linked behaviours and working on one's self. The purpose of all this was to achieve peace of mind.

G. Cambridge et al., *The Desistance Journey*,
https://doi.org/10.1007/978-3-031-11269-0_8

Keywords Masculinity · Violence · Hard man · Identity · Honest life

With some notable and fairly recent exceptions (i.e. Best & Colman, 2020; Chen, 2010; Marsh, 2011; Schroeder et al., 2007), the academic literature on desistance from crime and recovery from addiction have been produced separately. Some academics have, however, begun using 'social identity' frameworks to analyse both processes and in a way have brought the processes together (i.e. Best, 2019; Best et al., 2016; Frings & Albery, 2015; Kay & Monaghan, 2019). The narratives from interviews conducted for the present book align with elements of these social identity frameworks by emphasising that neither desistance nor recovery are linear processes and that both require identity change which can be facilitated by membership of new pro-social groups.

The literature that does attend to both desistance and recovery has tended to present the processes as related, although the relationship is constructed as hierarchical with desistance being subordinate to recovery (Best et al., 2017). The accounts of the men who participated in this research provide an in-depth insight into the inter-relatedness of the processes of desistance and recovery for a population of persisters who all experienced addiction. The themes that emerged from the analysis of the men's experiences strongly suggest that, for this population, desistance be conceived of as a side effect of recovery.

Multiple Childhood Traumas and Masculinity

A key theme running through all participants' life histories was their experience of childhood and teenage trauma. They all experienced economic deprivation, neglect, physical and emotional abuse, violence in the home and, parental problematic alcohol and drug use. Related to experiences of trauma was the dominance of the hard-man culture in the areas they were raised. Indeed, a key finding of this study was the overarching impact of culturally and historically informed identity heritage on the men's lifestyle, notably the influence of a specific form of hegemonic masculinity (Connell, 2005; also Dwyer, 2014). This hard-man identity valued risk taking, problematic drug and alcohol use, violence, aggression and toughness while avoiding displays of weakness and, devaluing education, legitimate employment and talking about emotions.

Many academic studies have identified such local cultures as originating in economic deprivation and social exclusion (Anderson, 1999; Bourgois, 1995; Hourigan, 2011; Windle, 2019, 2021; Winlow, 2001). Our participants' narratives are no different. Poverty was a key element of the mens' stories; all came from some of Ireland's most economically deprived areas. Some recounted surviving extreme poverty having to steal food at a young age to satiate their hunger, or stealing toys because they knew there would be no gifts at Christmas. Their poverty and home lives made school difficult. It's hard to concentrate if you're tired from staying awake while parents fight or party downstairs, or hungry because there's no food in the house. It's hard to stay in school if you're bullied by other students, and sometimes teachers, or if you feel ashamed of wearing uniforms which are old, dirty or worn. Being ridiculed for being poor and neglected and being punished for being poor and neglected, were common experiences for the men in this study. They all felt school was a lost opportunity for them to be *seen* and they spoke of school being the only place they could realistically have gotten help, but in most cases none was forthcoming. This is of course also a reflection on the lack of services available to support these children outside of the school setting and saying that none of the men spoke of local or state support agency involvement during their childhoods.

The men also recalled how the hard-man culture was passed down from generation to generation and that this form of masculinity was the only show in town. As a result, they lacked any alternative pro-social role models, so looked to those exhibiting hegemonic masculinity to guide their behaviour. The men looked up to those who had been to prison, could hold their drink and drugs, and had reputations for violence. As children, they wanted to emulate these men.

Importantly, not everyone from the RAPID areas of the city became addicted to alcohol or drugs or served time in prison. Our sample all had multiple convictions and experienced addiction over prolonged periods of time but still represent a very small minority of the people who live in these communities. In fact, our sample even represents a small proportion of the population who deal with addiction; importantly, as we know, the percentage of people who end up in prison is low, but those who persist in offending and experience addiction are over-represented in the system. The men who took part in this study were always at high risk of engaging in crime and experiencing addiction; that is not to say it was pre-determined, but the *risk* factors were present. As children, they were exposed to trauma, poverty, deprivation, lack of schooling, inadequate supervision, lack of services and often no ***one good adult*** in their lives. Alongside all of these risk factors, any combination of which may put someone on a path to addiction and offending, the men in this study enthusiastically internalised the norms and cultural expectations prioritised by the ***hard-men*** that ruled their families and neighbourhoods.

While their lifestyle reflected their peer group and was drawn from the local culture, it was also inherited from family members. Moreover, the men truly believed that they had to conform to these norms in order to survive. They believed (often justifiably so) that to display 'weakness', such as by talking about emotions or avoiding violence, would end with them being victimised. Being seen as weak opened them to becoming a victim themselves. With this lifestyle almost inevitably came problematic alcohol and drug use. Indeed, heavy drink and drug use was an expected part of the performance of masculinity for these men.

Adult Offending Was Founded Within Addiction

The men in this study had varied criminal careers. Some had repeat incarcerations for the same type of crime, and others undertook a range of offences. They spoke about how, as young men, they were initially motivated by any combination of thrill-seeking, peer pressure, boredom, economic deprivation and, most importantly, their drive to develop hard-man reputations: their offending was driven by their sense of masculinity, itself a response to economic deprivation and childhood trauma.

As the men aged and entered active addiction, their crimes became more directly linked to their addiction. That is, while most who offend as teenagers and young adults ***age out*** of crime as they mature (i.e. they stop offending), the men in this study persisted in offending due to their addiction. Most described being violent while intoxicated and/or committing crimes to fund their addiction. As they descended further into active addiction, the offending became more chaotic.

Experiencing Rock Bottoms and the Motivation to Find 'peace of mind'

As the men fell deeper and deeper into addiction, their mental and physical health deteriorated further, romantic and family relationships ended, and friends abandoned them. They often lost the highly valued and revered hard-man identity. Most had suicidal thoughts, many attempted suicide. The men talked about how, at this stage, they had two options: death or recovery—that they physically and emotionally could not continue as they were. They spoke of being physically and mentally tortured, and that seeking peace of mind was the ultimate motivator for change.

This descent along a rocky road to rock bottom was also a motivator for change. Avoiding an imagined future self or a 'feared self' (Paternoster & Bushway, 2009) was an important part of this process. The men feared what they were and might become, they often disliked themselves, and had already lost the self-identity which they had coveted—but when on this rocky road the future was even darker. The literature speaks about 'hooks for change' (Giordano et al., 2002), an influential concept for thinking about desistance, but this notion is only useful to a point. Hooks for change are opportunities for change that inspire individuals to attempt to desist. While some did identify parenthood as a hook which *started* them thinking about change, these approaches make a fundamental assumption that individuals actively and positively choose a path away from crime and then had the capacity to act on this choice. Whether the choices hinge on a rational assessment of their life or an avoidance of a negative future, this approach assumes agency in that decision. The men in this study, however, reported being forced to consider changing their lifestyle in the *absence* of options. Facing death, the individuals found themselves in a zero-sum scenarios—they could choose either recovery or die from overdose/suicide.

Once in treatment, positive role models became highly important, especially those who had successfully recovered from addiction and were seen to be living a stable and meaningful life. These individuals gave them hope that they too could achieve success. These role models were particularly important when they were from the same area and had similar life experiences. The men clearly emphasise, however, that making the decision to initially enter into, and fully engage with, recovery was very much inspired by avoidance of death—they do not recall any other motive at the time. Having role models helped them throughout the process, but it was seldom the impetus to first engage with treatment.

The point at which they entertained the option for change was the point at which they chose to seek recovery. Offending had little if anything to do with that decision, ultimately the men sought what they describe as 'peace of mind': they were tortured by their addiction and seeking peace was their focus. They understood their situation to be entirely tied to addiction, they saw recovery as the only way out, and they believed every other issue they were dealing with would improve as they recovered. Unlike desistance frameworks that focus on pro-social behaviour (Laub & Sampson, 2003) and the communal benefit of an individual stopping offending (Shapland & Bottoms, 2011), in addiction the focus is initially on the individual and their physical and mental well-being. While the men do recall having a future-orientated outlook regarding their recovery in terms of avoidance of death, the motive around the time they initially sought treatment was centred upon relief from the consequences of addiction. In addition, the focus was internal: there was seldom much reflection beyond their own experience, and an external outlook only came later into recovery.

Avoiding Gateway Behaviours

As the men progressed in their recovery, dealing with family, friends and support networks became more relevant. In the early phase of recovery, the men needed to isolate themselves from existing friends, and often family members, as well as their entire community. This was partly because of the influence of the street culture. This 'knifing off' (Maruna, 2001; Maruna & Roy, 2007) was primarily designed to avoid individuals who could derail their recovery. The temptation to use alcohol/drugs was often unmanageable when around old friends and acquaintances, as was the pressure to engage in 'gateway' activities. The men talked of trying to live an honest life, and how any deviation into activities that ran counter would put them at risk.

The men identified how the cultural interpretation of masculinity they experienced amongst old friends and families was directly in opposition to the process of recovery they were attempting to embrace. They had to avoid gateway behaviours linked to the old form of masculinity they coveted, including selling drugs, hanging around or being idle, short-term disrespectful relationships with women and being aggressive or violent. These linked behaviours, all associated with hegemonic masculinity, put their recovery at risk.

Some were initially unwilling, or unable, to let go of all linked behaviours. Some, for example, were attending 12-Step Meetings and treatment services, and had decided to not use heroin, but continued smoking cannabis. They relapsed. The men had little tolerance for gateway behaviours and to engage in such would, and often did, lead them back to active addiction.

The Importance of New Relationships and New Role Models

The process of knifing off (Maruna, 2001; Maruna & Roy, 2007) was central to the process of recovery as described in this study. It was the first step in what ultimately became the rejection of the social identity that influenced the men's behaviour. This was, however, a catch-22 situation for the men in this study. Avoidance of friends and family left them isolated, alone and vulnerable in a very unstable period in their recovery. Without a *replacement* social group—without that reference group upon which to build their new social identity through interpersonal interaction—the men could never progress to ultimately achieving a new identity compatible with sobriety and non-offending.

While much of the desistance literature highlights the importance of relationships for desistance (i.e. Healy, 2012; McAlinden et al., 2017; McNeil et al., 2012) the men needed new relationships in order to progress. They could seldom rely on existing friendships. As such, the role of recovery groups such as AA/NA and sponsor programmes were vital (also Best, 2019; Best et al., 2016; Kay & Monaghan, 2019). These groups served a multitude of purposes including, by default, facilitating desistance from crime. The groups served as new friendship networks, modelled appropriate behaviour, modelled new ways of being a man, offered a new pro-social identity and, provided structure and meaning to their day.

Some reported seeing friends, family and people they had been incarcerated with in recovery. These people were good role models for them. They showed the men that there was a way out of the devastation their addiction was causing to their lives, modelled that they too could change. Some of the men imitated what these men were doing, which helped them during their journey into recovery. The role of role models had come full circle: the men had often started heavy drinking and drug taking, and engaging in violence, because those they looked up to as young men were doing the same. Now they were in recovery, they looked up to those who had accepted new forms of masculinity and were living new lives.

The Importance of Community

The process of engaging in recovery groups relieved the significant void left by knifing off (see Marsh, 2011): it allowed the development of new social bonds in the context of a recovery community. Nugent and Schinkel (2016) point out that the isolation of knifing off can prevent the formation of a new identity, and can thus be a barrier to desistance. This transition phase, what Healy (2012) calls a liminal space between criminal and mainstream society, is a period of great instability but also a key element of both desistance and recovery. Identity shift is a necessary process in most desistance schools of thought—from rational choice (Paternoster & Bushway, 2009) to narrative approaches (Maruna, 2001)—and central to most models of recovery from addiction (Best, 2019; Best et al., 2016; Kay & Monaghan, 2019).

The men's account of the process also points to the importance of constructing a new social identity, and through interpersonal interaction, this social identity informs the development of the self-concept (Best, 2016; Best et al., 2016). The shearing from past reference groups, sometimes including family, was a necessary precondition to the creation of a new sense of self. This highlights the importance of identity as a socially negotiated and constructed phenomenon for the men.

This phase of change is a vulnerable period for individuals in recovery, and relapse is common. The realisation that recovery involves a fundamental reordering of one's life and ideas about life, a re-evaluation of one's history, identity, culture and beliefs is an exceptionally daunting experience. Many of the men did trip up during this phase, but all learned from their relapse, and tried again.

The Role of Paid Employment

The rich description that emerged in the data collected for this project served to elucidate the process of recovery and desistance but also highlighted how certain process frameworks are inaccurate in the case of substance using desisters. For example, there is an emphasis in the academic literature on employment as a means of informal social control, through introducing structure and meaning into an individual's life and supporting new identities based on the development of new social bonds (Laub & Sampson, 2001, 2003).

For the men in this study, however, employment was often well out of their reach. Not only did having a criminal record prevent the men from gaining meaningful or even any employment (see Farrall et al., 2014; Leonard, 2021), they were hampered in their job search by poor social skills, inabilities to cope with stress and, the emotional and physical effects of addiction, trauma and poor mental health. Employment in the early months of recovery may only serve to push individuals back into active addiction. This is not to say that employment was not an option and many did find employment eventually, but the men did not have the necessary skills required to enter the job market in the short- to medium term, nor did they initially find employment beneficial in terms of meaning making, identity and recovery (see Skardhamar & Savolainen, 2014). Most importantly, the men needed to spend significant amounts of time working on their own issues, both mental and physical, in order to arrive at a place where they were resilient enough to cope with the strains of day-to-day life without using drugs/drink.

The Importance of Mental Health Care and Identity Change

Dealing with poor mental health was a challenge for all of the men in this study. *All* of the participants reported having experienced multiple adverse experiences when they were younger, including poverty, physical abuse, sexual abuse, domestic violence, addiction in the home, and/or neglect. The men also experienced significant trauma during their lifetime. They were victims of crime, they experienced homelessness, overdosed on drugs, attempted suicide and, suffered the death of friends and family. Even being perpetrators of violence, as all of the men were, has been shown to be traumatic for young people, with some young violent offenders presenting with PTSD in the aftermath of engaging in interpersonal violence (Beresford & Wood, 2016). Prior to attempting recovery, the men had not confronted these events, nor processed them, but had self-medicated with their chosen substance. As such, the decision to enter recovery was a difficult journey into self-reflection and a willingness to deal with their past.

While working on themselves, the men learned who they wanted to be and what their identity could be without using drink/drugs. They developed a narrative that reinforced the belief that they were a fundamentally good person who was waylaid, because of their addiction (Marsh, 2011;

Maruna, 2001). This was very important for the participants because it offered them a means of rationalising past behaviours and accepting themselves as they were now. Self-preservation was necessary to allow them to deal with their past and look to their future: the burden of past behaviours needed to be lessened for them to progress. By pointing to addiction as the context of their behaviour they were able to (in some part) assign blame outside of themselves. This allowed them to construct a narrative whereby they were always a fundamentally 'good' person but the circumstances made them 'bad'. The logic was that it was their addiction that made them do the things they did. With the removal of drink/drugs the men were able to start their journey into recovery and learn new ways to live. With this approach to their sense of self, identity and taking responsibility for past behaviours, recovery served a number of purposes—it removed the *cause* of their anti-social and self-harming behaviour, it offered them a base to begin considering a more pro-social existence and it protected them from having the entirety of the weight of their past transgressions directly on their shoulders. None denied responsibility for their past actions, but not identifying a cause for this behaviour would have made change near impossible.

Stages of Rehabilitation and Desistance

Maruna and Farrall's (2004) primary and secondary desistance and McNeill's (2016) tertiary desistance, provide a good understanding of the stages or phases of desistance (a process which is never linear). For the men, primary desistance often started while they were in prison. Some continued on this recovery journey when they came out to the community and others relapsed and began the cycle again. Some initially had what might be called a partial commitment to recovery and desistance, which usually involved abstaining from a drug/alcohol but not totally breaking away from the problem-linked behaviours (the gateway behaviours). This approach always eventually ended in relapse. Avoiding relapse required them to identify, change and avoid all of their gateway behaviours. None of these changes happened overnight. It took some of the men in this study many years to change their attitudes and behaviours: it often took relapses and support for the men to identify what their gateway behaviours were.

The process of identity change fits with the definition of secondary desistance. While in recovery the men reflected on how they very slowly changed their outlook, self-perception and social identity. They described this as a process of discovery. They talked of stripping away hegemonic masculinity and becoming their raw selves without the masks of drugs, alcohol or violence. They reflected on this process as a particularly difficult time—they had to completely step back from the life they once knew and, worst of all, step away from their friends, family and community. The process of *rebuilding* was made possible through networks of support linked to addiction support organisations. One participant commentated that he did not know how 'non-addicts' desisted—how could they change without recovery programmes.

Reintroduction to society was a final phase of the recovery process that the men experienced. For most of the men, this process occurred many months (and sometimes years) into their recovery journey. Reintroduction took a number of forms and happened in a number of settings. Many slowly reconnected with family and friends, although some continued to avoid those who threatened their recovery. The men also experienced a phase of reintroduction within the community: some had a difficult time being accepted back. Society at large can find it very difficult to trust people who have been to prison and are recovering from addiction (Giordano et al., 2002; Leonard, 2021; Maruna, 2001; Paternoster & Bushway, 2009). This can complicate the development of a new social identity that the individual sees as separate from their past identity. Not being accepted, or having one's identity denied, can prevent a meaningful reconnection to society. This can be enough for some to give up on their desistance/recovery journey, as they see themselves as 'doomed to deviance' (Maruna, 2001).

You Cannot Have Desistance Without Recovery

The scant literature on the link between recovery and desistance suggests that not only is there a link between addiction and offending, but that amongst men like those who participated in this study desistance from offending is subordinate to recovery from addiction (Roeyen et al., 2017, see Colman & Vander Laenen, 2012; Marsh, 2011; McCray et al., 2011). The narratives presented in this book show, however, the importance of dealing with desistance and recovery as processes that are so intertwined that they cannot be separated. You cannot have desistance without recovery and, for the men in this study, you cannot have a meaningful recovery without desistance.

There is a recognition in the academic literature that the type of offence impacts the process of desistance. For example, we know that individuals who commit terrorism offences or sexual assaults have a different trajectory into and through desistance (i.e. Cresswell, 2021; Lynch, 2015). This book advocates, however, that the type of crime is less relevant than addiction and, trauma, economic deprivation and masculinity. The men in this study felt they had no alternative but to behave in a particular way to ensure their survival. Surviving on the streets meant projecting the hard-man identity and adhering to social norms that in other circumstances would be seen as deviant. The social pressure, the family and tribal obligations felt by the men and the cultural norms they grew up with all coalesced to ensure the men felt they had limited choices and a pre-determined fate.

Changing Conceptions of Hegemonic Masculinity Can Help Both Desistance and Recovery

Everyone experiences recovery differently. Some individuals achieve recovery on their first attempt, others need numerous attempts; some might never make it, some will die trying. The life experience of people attempting recovery influences this process. An important element in understanding the process of recovery and desistance is to work with the skills and resilience that the individual possesses, this is called a strengths-based approach. Individuals like the men in this study experienced profoundly traumatic childhoods and lived chaotic lives—as a result they possessed few useful coping skills when it came to desisting and recovery. This impacted them in terms of the intervention needed and the duration, and the likelihood of relapse.

We advocate here another way to look at desistance/recovery that is relevant for people in active addiction by incorporating our understanding of hegemonic masculinity into the recovery and desistance processes. Carlsson (2013) highlights how the processes of persistence and desistance are linked with age-specific norms of what it means to 'be a man' and how individuals successfully 'do masculinity' in different stages of life. That is, masculinity can be linked to delinquency during adolescence, but can encourage desistance during the transition stage to adulthood. Criminal behaviour explained as an expression of 'being a man' during adolescence can, in some cases, be seen as incompatible with the idea of 'being a man' in adulthood (Massoglia & Uggen, 2010; Moffit, 1993).

That is, most people recognise what are age-appropriate ways of 'doing masculinity' and also the impact of hegemonic masculinity on their own well-being, however, many of the men in this study did not recognise this until well into the recovery process. Helping those in active addiction recognise this, and shift their ideas of what it is to be a man will help them progress. The recognition of the historic and cultural manifestations of masculinity can also be vital in developing a critical awareness of the origins of their problem behaviours—it provides them another tool to identify why they behaved as they did. It supports their narrative that they are, deep down, a good person constrained by circumstances beyond their control.

This is, however, but one part of the process. For the men interviewed in this research their whole identity was formed around the notion of being *tough*. This identity was linked to survival for men growing up in economically deprived and socially excluded parts of the city. In their neighbourhood (and in prison) the people who were respected were the people who could 'look after themselves', those with the ability and willingness to fight, or at least 'have a go'. Fear, intimidation, and fighting are key survival strategies. Those did not fit the masculine stereotypes and were unwilling to use violence, could become victims of violence (see Anderson, 1999; Windle & Briggs, 2015). Decades of research have shown that these conceptions of masculinity are born of economic deprivation and social exclusion—that men search for respect and power when legitimate options have been denied (see Anderson, 1999; Bourgois, 1995; Carlsson, 2013; Tomsen, 2008; Windle, 2019).

The hard-man image did not leave the men straight away—they had cultivated the image, maintained it and lived with it for many years. It had also served to protect them on the street and in prison. While understandably slow to let this image and performance go, they did identify their addiction as negative and, whilst in recovery, started to reconfigure what it meant to be a man in a more—pro-social way (see Bendelow & Williams, 2005; Dwyer, 2014).

This study has challenged some constructions of desistance in the literature. It has raised the possibility that, in the case of addiction, desistance emerges as a side effect of recovery. In addition, the life stories of the men in this study point to the importance of historically and culturally transmitted manifestations of masculinity in shaping the behaviour choices that ultimately lead to active addiction. Consequently, the data suggests that we must address issues of hegemonic masculinity, calling out cultures that prioritise violence, risk taking and bravado. We must challenge identities that are intimately linked to the kinds of masculinity prioritised in adolescence—these are all issues that are fundamental to achieving recovery and desistance. Challenging these identities require, however, more than words—these identities are founded in economic deprivation and social exclusion, and passed down from each generation. Longer term policies must focus on reducing inequalities.

Furthermore, in the words of one of the men, in order to recover and desist you have to live an *honest life*. Not doing crime, not consuming drugs or alcohol, is not success. For the men in this study, being kind, thoughtful and introspective and contributing to society were key parts of the process. The path to success was about honesty, avoiding problematic linked behaviours, working on one's self. The purpose of all this was to achieve peace of mind.

References

Anderson, E. (1999). *Code of the street: Decency, violence, and the moral life of the inner city*. Norton.

Bendelow, G., & Williams, S. J. (2005). *Emotions in social life: Critical themes and contemporary issues*. Routledge.

Beresford, H., & Wood, J. L. (2016). Patients or perpetrators? The effects of trauma exposure on gang members' mental health: A review of the literature. *Journal of Criminological Research, Policy and Practice, 17*(3), 223–246.

Best, D. (2016). Social identity, social networks and social capital in desistance and recovery. In A. Robinson & P. Hamilton (Eds.), *Moving on from crime and substance use: Transforming identities* (pp. 175–186). Policy Press.

Best, D. (2019). *Pathways to recovery and desistance*. Policy.

Best, D., & Colman, C. (2020). *Strengths-based approaches to crime and substance use: From drugs and crime to desistance and recovery*. Routledge.

Best, D., Beckwith, M., Haslam, S., Haslam, A., Jetten, J., Mawson, E., & Lubman, D. (2016). Overcoming alcohol and other drug addiction as a process of social identity transition: The social identity model of recovery (SIMOR). *Addiction Research and Theory, 24*(2), 111–123.

Best, D., Irving, J., & Albertson, K. (2017). Recovery and desistance: What the emerging recovery movement in the alcohol and drug area can learn from models of desistance from offending. *Addiction Theory and Research, 25*(1), 1–10.

Bourgois, P. (1995). *In search of respect: Selling crack in El Barrio*. Cambridge University Press.

Carlsson, C. (2013). Masculinities, persistence and desistence. *Criminology, 51*(3), 661–693.
Chen, G. (2010). The meaning of suffering in drug addiction and recovery from the perspective of existentialism, Buddhism and the 12-step program. *Journal of Psychoactive Drugs, 42*(3), 363–375.
Colman, C., & Vander Laenen, F. (2012). 'Recovery came first': Desistance versus recovery in the criminal careers of drug-using offenders. *Scientific World Journal, 2012*, 1–9.
Connell, R. R. (2005). *Masculinities*. Polity.
Cresswell, C. (2021). Giving voice to convicted perpetrators of sexual harm: Assisted desistance in the community. In O. Lynch, J. Windle, & Y. Ahmed (Eds.), *Giving voice to diversity in criminological research: Nothing about us without us* (pp. 209–233). Policy.
Dwyer, D. (2014). The lived experiences of men in 12-step recovery against a backdrop of hegemonic masculinity. *Irish Probation Journal, 11*(1), 177–195.
Farrall, S., Hunter, B., Sharpe, G., & Calverley, A. (2014). *Criminal careers in transition*. Oxford University Press.
Frings, D., & Albery, I. P. (2015). The social identity model of cessation maintenance: Formulation and initial evidence. *Addictive Behaviors, 44*(1), 35–42.
Giordano, P. C., Cernkovich, S. A., & Rudolph, J. L. (2002). Gender, crime, and desistance: Toward a theory of cognitive transformation. *American Journal of Sociology, 107*(2), 990–1064.
Healy, D. (2012). *The dynamics of desistance: Charting pathways through change*. Routledge.
Hourigan, N. (2011). *Understanding limerick*. Cork University Press.
Kay, C., & Monaghan, M. (2019). Rethinking recovery and desistance processes: Developing a social identity model of transition. *Addiction Research and Theory, 27*(1), 47–54.
Laub, J. H., & Sampson, R. J. (2001). Understanding desistance from crime. *Crime and Justice, 28*(1), 1–69.
Laub, J. H., & Sampson, R. J. (2003). *Shared beginnings, divergent lives: Delinquent boys to age 70*. Harvard University Press.
Leonard, J. (2021). An autobiographical account of desistance and recovery. In Lynch, O., Windle, J., & Ahmed, Y. (Eds.), *Giving voice to diversity in criminological research: Nothing about us without us* (pp. 149–156). Policy.
Lynch, O. (2015). Desistance and de radicalization—The case of terrorism and political violence. In S. Zeiger & A. Aly (Eds.), *Countering violent extremism: Developing an evidence base for policy and practice*. Curtin University Press.
Marsh, B. (2011). Narrating desistance: Identity change and the 12-step script. *Irish Probation Journal, 8*(1), 49–68.

Maruna, S. (2001). *Making good: How ex-convicts reform and rebuild their lives*. American Psychological Association Press.

Maruna, S., & Farrall, S. (2004). Desistance from crime: A theoretical reformulation. *Kolner Zeitschrift Fur Soziologie Und Sozialpsychologie, 43*(2), 171–194.

Maruna, S., & Roy, K. (2007). Amputation or reconstruction? Notes on 'knifing off' and desistance from crime. *Journal of Contemporary Criminal Justice, 23*(1), 104–124.

Massoglia, M., & Uggen, C. (2010). Settling down and aging out: Towards an interactionist theory of desistence and the transition to adulthood. *American Journal of Sociology, 116*(2), 543–582.

McAlinden, A. M., Farmer, M., & Maruna, S. (2017). Desistance from sexual offending: Do the mainstream theories apply? *Criminology and Criminal Justice, 17*(3), 266–283.

McCray, K., Wesely, J. K., & Rasche, C. E. (2011). Rehab retrospect: Former prostitutes and the (re)construction of deviance. *Deviant Behavior, 32*(8), 743–768.

McNeill, F. (2006). Community supervision: Context and relationships matter. In B. Goldson & J. Muncie (Eds.), *Youth crime and justice* (pp. 125–139). Sage.

McNeill, F., Farrall, S., Lightowler, C., & Maruna, S. (2012). *How and why people stop offending: Discovering desistance*. IRISS.

Moffit, T. (1993). Adolescence-limited and life course persistent anti-social behaviour; a development taxonomy. *Psychological Review, 100*(4), 674–701.

Nugent, B., & Schinkel, M. (2016). The pains of desistance. *Criminology and Criminal Justice, 16*(5), 568–584.

Paternoster, R., & Bushway, S. (2009). Desistance and the "feared self": Toward an identity theory of criminal desistance. *The Journal of Criminal Law and Criminology, 99*(3), 1103–1156.

Roeyen, S. V., Anderson, S., Vanderplasschen, W., Colman, C., & Vander Laenen, F. (2017). Desistance in drug-using offenders: A narrative review. *European Journal of Criminology, 14*(5), 606–625.

Schroeder, R. D., Giordano, P. C., & Cernkovich, S. A. (2007). Drug use and desistance processes. *Criminology, 45*(10), 191–198.

Shapland, J., & Bottoms, A. (2011). Reflections on social values, offending and desistance among young adult recidivists. *Punishment and Society, 13*(3), 256–282.

Skardhamar, T., & Savolainen, J. (2014). Changes in criminal offending around the time of job entry: A study of employment and desistance. *Criminology, 52*(2), 263–291.

Tomsen, S. (2008). Masculinities, crime, and criminalisation. In T. Anthony & C. Cunneen (Eds.), *Theoretical criminology companion* (pp. 94–104). Hawkins Press.

Windle, J. (2019). The causes and consequences of gangland violence in the Republic of Ireland. In R. Lombardo (Ed.), *Organized crime: Causes and consequences* (pp. 110–123). Nova Science.

Windle, J. (2021). Reconsidering the 1991 Blackbird Leys Rioters as an underclass: An insider perspective. In O. Lynch, J. Windle, & Y. Ahmed (Eds.), *Giving voice to diversity in criminological research: Nothing about us without us* (pp. 133–148). Policy.

Windle, J., & Briggs, D. (2015). Going solo: The social organisation of drug dealing within a London street gang. *Journal of Youth Studies, 18*(9), 1170–1185.

Winlow, S. (2001). *Badfellas crime, tradition and new masculinities*. Berg.

References

Abrantes, A. M., Brown, S. A., & Tomlinson, K. L. (2004). Psychiatric comorbidity among inpatient substance abusing adolescents. *Journal of Child and Adolescent Substance Abuse, 13*(2), 83–101.

Aguiler, J. L. (1981). Insider research: An ethnography of a debate. In D. A. Messerschmidt (Ed.), *Anthropologists at home in North America* (pp. 15–26). Cambridge University Press.

Ahmed, E., Harris, N., Braithwaite, J., & Braithwaite, V. (2001). *Shame management through reintegration*. Cambridge University Press.

Allen, K. (2000). *The celtic tiger: The myth of social partnership*. Manchester University Press.

Allen, M., Donohue, W. A., Griffin, A., Ryan, D., & Turner, M. (2003). Comparing the influence of parents and peers on the choice to use drugs: A meta-analytic summary of the literature. *Criminal Justice and Behavior, 30*(2), 163–186.

Anderson, E. (1999). *Code of the street: Decency, violence, and the moral life of the inner city*. Norton.

Asselin, M. E. (2003). Insider research: Issues to consider when doing qualitative research in your own setting. *Journal for Nurses in Professional Development, 19*(2), 99–103.

Bacik, I., & O'Connell, M. (1998). *Crime and poverty in Ireland*. Round Hall.

Bell, J. (2005). *Doing your research project*. Open University Press.

Bendelow, G., & Williams, S. J. (2005). *Emotions in social life: Critical themes and contemporary issues*. Routledge.

Bennett, T., & Holloway, K. (2005). *Understanding drugs, alcohol and crime*. McGraw-Hill.

G. Cambridge et al., *The Desistance Journey*,
https://doi.org/10.1007/978-3-031-11269-0

Bennett, T., Holloway, K., & Farrington, D. (2008). The statistical association between drug misuse and crime: A meta-analysis. *Aggression and Violent Behaviour, 13*(2), 107–118.

Best, D. (2016). Social identity, social networks and social capital in desistance and recovery. In A. Robinson & P. Hamilton (Eds.), *Moving on from crime and substance use: Transforming identities* (pp. 175–186). Policy Press.

Best, D. (2019). *Pathways to recovery and desistance*. Policy.

Best, D., & Colman, C. (2020). *Strengths-based approaches to crime and substance use: From drugs and crime to desistance and recovery*. Routledge.

Best, D., & Savic, M. (2015). Substance abuse and offending. Pathways to recovery. In R. Sheehan & J. Ogloff (Eds.), *Working within the forensic paradigm: Cross-discipline approaches for policy and practice* (pp. 259–271). Routledge.

Best, D., Beckwith, M., Haslam, S., Haslam, A., Jetten, J., Mawson, E., & Lubman, D. (2016). Overcoming alcohol and other drug addiction as a process of social identity transition: The social identity model of recovery (SIMOR). *Addiction Research and Theory, 24*(2), 111–123.

Best, D., Irving, J., & Albertson, K. (2017). Recovery and desistance: What the emerging recovery movement in the alcohol and drug area can learn from models of desistance from offending. *Addiction Theory and Research, 25*(1), 1–10.

Betty Ford Institute Consensus Panel. (2007). What is recovery? A working definition from the Betty Ford Institute. *Journal of Substance Abuse Treatment, 33*(3), 221–228.

Beresford, H., & Wood, J. L. (2016). Patients or perpetrators? The effects of trauma exposure on gang members' mental health: A review of the literature. *Journal of Criminological Research, Policy and Practice, 17*(3), 223–246.

Blokland, A. A., & Palmen, H. (2012). Criminal career patterns. In R. Loeber, M. Hoeve, N. W. Slot, & P. van der Laan (Eds.), *Persisters and desisters in crime from adolescence into adulthood* (pp. 13–50). Routledge.

Bonner, A., & Tolhurst, G. (2002). Insider-outsider perspectives of participant observation. *Nurse Researcher, 9*(4), 7–19.

Bourgois, P. (1995). *In search of respect: Selling crack in El Barrio*. Cambridge University Press.

Brannigan, R., Schackman, B. R., Falco, M., & Millman, R. B. (2004). The quality of highly regarded adolescent substance abuse treatment programs: Results of an in-depth national survey. *Archives of Paediatrics and Adolescent Medicine, 158*(4), 904–909.

Bruguera, P., Reynolds, J., Gilvarry, E., Braddick, F., Marath-Veettil, A. L., Anderson, P., & Gual, A. (2018). How does economic recession affect substance use? A reality check with clients of drug treatment centres. *The Journal of Mental Health Policy and Economics, 21*(1), 11–16.

Brunt, B. (1988). The new industrialization of Ireland. In R. Carter & A. J. Parker (Eds.), *Ireland: A contemporary geographical perspective* (pp. 115–131). Routledge.

Campbell, B. (1993). *Goliath: Britain's dangerous places*. Methuen.

Callan, T., Nolan, B., Keane, C., Savage, M., & Walsh, J. (2013). The Great Recession, austerity and inequality: Evidence from Ireland. *Intereconomics, 48*(6), 335–338.

Carlsson, C. (2012). Using 'turning points' to understand processes of change in offending: Notes from a Swedish study on life courses and crime. *The British Journal of Criminology, 52*(1), 1–16.

Carlsson, C. (2013). Masculinities, persistence and desistence. *Criminology, 51*(3), 661–693.

Changing the Narrative. (n.d.). *Words matter*. https://www.changingthenarrative.news/stigmatizing-language

CSO (Central Statistics Office). (2011). *This is Ireland, Census 2011*. http://www.cso.ie/en/census/census2011reports/census2011thisisirelandpart1/

CSO (Central Statistics Office). (2016). *This is Ireland, Census 2016*. https://www.cso.ie/en/census/census2016reports/

Charmaz, K. (2006). *Constructing grounded theory: A practical guide through qualitative analysis*. Sage.

Chavez, C. (2008). Conceptualizing from the inside: Advantages, complications, and demands on insider positionality. *The Qualitative Report, 13*(3), 474–494.

Chen, G. (2010). The meaning of suffering in drug addiction and recovery from the perspective of existentialism, Buddhism and the 12-step program. *Journal of Psychoactive Drugs, 42*(3), 363–375.

Chen, G. (2018). Building recovery capital: The role of hitting bottom in desistance and recovery from substance abuse and crime. *Journal of Psychoactive Drugs, 50*(5), 420–419.

Cicchetti, D., & Toth, S. L. (1995). Developmental psychopathology and disorders of affect. In D. Cicchetti & D. J. Cohen (Eds.), *Developmental Psychopathology* (pp. 369–420). John Wiley.

Coghlan, D. (2003). Practitioner research for organizational knowledge: Mechanistic- and organistic-oriented approaches to insider action research. *Management Learning, 34*(4), 451–463.

Colman, C., & Vander Laenen, F. (2012). 'Recovery came first': Desistance versus recovery in the criminal careers of drug-using offenders. *Scientific World Journal, 2012*, 1–9.

Committee Report. (1979). *Letter to clerk to joint committee from Cork corporation*.http://archive.oireachtas.ie/1980/APPENDIX_02101980_6.html

Connell, R. (2005). *Masculinities*. Polity.

Connell, R. W., & Messerschmidt, J. W. (2005). Hegemonic masculinity: Rethinking the concept. *Gender and Society, 19*(6), 829–859.

Cork City Council. (2020). *Cork city socio-economic summary profile.* https://www.corkcity.ie/en/media-folder/cork-city-development-plan/socio-economic-summary-profile.pdf

Costerly, C., Gibbs, P., & Elliott, G. C. (2010). *Doing work based research: Approaches to enquiry for insider-researchers*. Sage.

Coyle, B. (2019). 'What the f** k Is Maturity?': Young adulthood, subjective maturity and desistance from crime. *The British Journal of Criminology, 59*(5), 1178–1198.

Cresswell, C. (2021). Giving voice to convicted perpetrators of sexual harm: Assisted desistance in the community. In O. Lynch, J. Windle, & Y. Ahmed (Eds.), *Giving voice to diversity in criminological research: Nothing about us without us* (pp. 209–233). Policy.

Crewe, B., & Levins, A. (2019). The prison as a reinventive institution. *Theoretical Criminology, 24*(4), 568–589.

Crowley, J., Devoy, R., Linehan, D., & O'Flanagan, P. (2005). *Atlas of Cork city*. Cork University Press.

Darcy, C. (2020). Men and the drug buzz: Masculinity and men's motivations for illicit recreational drug use. *Sociological Research Online, 25*(3), 421–437.

Dillon, L. (2001). *Drug use among prisoners: An exploratory study*. The Health Research Board.

Dolan, A. (2011). 'You can't ask for a Dubonnet and lemonade!': Working class masculinity and men's health practices. *Sociology of Health and Illness, 33*(4), 586–601.

Dong, M., Anda, R. F., Felitti, V. J., Dube, S. R., Williamson, D. F., Thompson, T. J., Loo, C. M., & Giles, W. H. (2004). The interrelatedness of multiple forms of childhood abuse, neglect, and household dysfunction. *Child Abuse and Neglect, 28*(7), 771–784.

Dube, S. R., Felitti, V. J., Dong, M., Chapman, D. P., Giles, W. H., & Anda, R. F. (2003). Childhood abuse, neglect, and household dysfunction and the risk of illicit drug use: The adverse childhood experiences study. *Pediatrics, 111*(3), 564–572.

DuPont, R. L., & McGovern, J. P. (1992). Suffering in addiction: Alcoholism and drug dependence. In P. L. Starck & J. P. McGovern (Eds.), *The hidden dimension of illness: Human suffering* (pp. 155–201). National League for Nursing Press.

Dwyer, D. (2014). The lived experiences of men in 12-step recovery against a backdrop of hegemonic masculinity. *Irish Probation Journal, 11*(1), 177–195.

EMCDDA (European Monitoring Centre for Drugs and Drug Addiction). (2014). *European drug report (2014)*. http://www.emcdda.europa.eu/edr2014

EMCDDA (European Monitoring Centre for Drugs and Drug Addiction). (2020). *Problem drug use*. https://www.emcdda.europa.eu/topics/problem-drug-use_en

Etherington, K. (2009). Life story research: A relevant methodology for counsellors and psychotherapists. *Counselling and Psychotherapy Research, 9*(4), 225–233.

Farrall, S. (2005). On the existential aspects of desistance from crime. *Symbolic Interaction, 28*(3), 367–386.

Farrall, S. (2019). *The architecture of desistance*. Routledge.

Farrall, S., Hunter, B., Sharpe, G., & Calverley, A. (2014). *Criminal careers in transition*. Oxford University Press.

Farrington, D. (2007). Advancing knowledge about desistance. *Journal of Contemporary Criminal Justice, 23*(1), 125–134.

Fisher, J. (2000). Addictions and trauma recovery. *Paper presented at the International Society for the Study of Dissociation*. https://janinafisher.com/pdfs/addictions.pdf

Flynn, A., McDonald, N., & O'Doherty, F. (1967). A survey of boys in St. Patrick's Institution. *Irish Jurist, 2*(1), 222–232.

Ford, K., Bellis, M. A., Hughes, K., Barton, E. R., & Newbury, A. (2020). Adverse childhood experiences: A retrospective study to understand their associations with lifetime mental health diagnosis, self-harm or suicide attempt, and current low mental wellbeing in a male Welsh prison population. *Health and Justice, 8*(1), 1–13.

Fox, B. H., Perez, N., Cass, E., Baglivio, M. T., & Epps, N. (2015). Trauma changes everything: Examining the relationship between adverse childhood experiences and serious, violent and chronic juvenile offenders. *Child Abuse and Neglect, 46*(2), 163–173.

Freyd, J., Klest, B., & Allard, C. (2005). Betrayal trauma: Relationship to physical health, psychological distress, and a written disclosure intervention. *Journal of Trauma and Dissociation, 6*(3), 83–104.

Frings, D., & Albery, I. P. (2015). The social identity model of cessation maintenance: Formulation and initial evidence. *Addictive Behaviors, 44*(1), 35–42.

Giordano, P. C., Cernkovich, S. A., & Rudolph, J. L. (2002). Gender, crime, and desistance: Toward a theory of cognitive transformation. *American Journal of Sociology, 107*(2), 990–164.

Giordano, P. C., Schroeder, R. D., & Cernkovich, S. A. (2007). Emotions and crime over the life course: A neo-Meadian perspective on criminal continuity and change. *American Journal of Sociology, 112*(6), 1603–1661.

Goffman, E. (1967). *Interaction ritual: Essays on face-to-face interaction*. Aldine.

Graham, H. (2016). *Rehabilitation work: Supporting desistance and recovery*. Routledge.

Griffin, M., & Kelleher, P. (2010). Uncertain futures: Men on the margins in Limerick city. *Irish Probation Journal, 7*(1), 24–46.

Gunter, A. (2017). *Race, gangs and youth violence: Policy, prevention and policing*. Policy Press.

Healy, D. (2012). *The dynamics of desistance: Charting pathways through change*. Routledge.

Healy, D. (2016). 'I've always tried but I hadn't got the willpower': Understanding pathways to desistance in the Republic of Ireland. In J. Shapland, S. Farrall, & A. Bottoms (Eds.), *Global perspectives on desistance: Reviewing what we know and looking to the future* (pp. 50–65). Routledge.

Healy, D., & O'Donnell, I. (2008). Calling time on crime: Motivation, generativity and agency in Irish probationers. *Probation Journal, 55*(1), 25–38.

Healy, S., & Reynolds, B. (1990). *Work, unemployment and job-creation policy*. CORI Justice Commission.

Hirschi, T. (1969). *Causes of delinquency*. University of California Press.

Hobbs, D. (2001). The firm. Organizational logic and criminal culture on a shifting terrain. *British Journal of Criminology, 41*(4), 549–560.

Hourihan, K. (1979). The Cork land use and transportation study. *Irish Geography, 12*(1), 99–104.

Hourigan, N. (2011). *Understanding Limerick*. Cork University Press.

Hourigan, N., Morrison, J. F., Windle, J., & Silke, A. (2018). Crime in Ireland north and south: Feuding gangs and profiteering paramilitaries. *Trends in Organized Crime, 21*(2), 126–146.

Hser, Y. I. (1997). Drug treatment careers: A conceptual framework and existing research findings. *Journal of Substance Abuse Treatment, 14*(6), 543–558.

Ilan, J. (2015). *Understanding street culture: Poverty, crime, youth and cool*. Macmillan.

IPRT (Irish Penal Reform Trust). (2012). *The vicious circle of social exclusion and crime*. https://www.iprt.ie/site/assets/files/6264/position_paper_final.pdf

Irish Prison Service. (2013). *Irish prison service recidivism study*. https://www.irishprisons.ie/images/pdf/recidivismstudyss2.pdf

Irving, J. (2016). Alcoholics anonymous: Sustaining behavioural change. In A. Robinson & P. Hamilton (Eds.), *Moving on from crime and substance use: Transforming identities*. Policy.

Kandel, D., & Chen, K. (2000). Types of marijuana users by longitudinal course. *Journal of Studies on Alcohol, 61*(3), 367–378.

Katz, J. (1988). *Seductions of crime*. Basic Books.

Kay, C., & Monaghan, M. (2019). Rethinking recovery and desistance processes: Developing a social identity model of transition. *Addiction Research and Theory, 27*(1), 47–54.

Kelly, E., & McGuinness, S. (2015). Impact of the Great Recession on unemployed and NEET individuals' labour market transitions in Ireland. *Economic Systems, 39*(1), 59–71.

Kelly, T., & Hayes, P. (2014). *Cork city profile. A statistical and geographical profile of Cork city local authority area focused on health and social inclusion*. Cork Healthy Cities and Social Inclusion Unit.

Kennedy Report. (1970). *Reformatory and industrial schools systems report*. The Stationary Office.

Kilkelly, U. (2006). Operationalising children's rights: Lessons from research. *Journal of Children's Services, 1*(4), 35–46.

Kirby, P. (2002). *Reinventing Ireland*. Pluto.

Kleiman, M. A., Caulkins, J. P., & Hawken, A. (2011). *Drugs and drug policy: What everyone needs to know*. Oxford University Press.

Kupers, T. A. (2005). Toxic masculinity as a barrier to mental health treatment in prison. *Journal of Clinical Psychology, 61*(6), 713–724.

Lambert, S., & Gill-Emerson, G. (2017). *ACEs at Cork Simon: Exploring the connection between early trauma and later negative life events among Cork Simon service users*. Simon Community.

Laub, J. H., & Sampson, R. J. (2001). Understanding desistance from crime. *Crime and Justice, 28*(1), 1–69.

Laub, J. H., & Sampson, R. J. (2003). *Shared beginnings, divergent lives: Delinquent boys to age 70*. Harvard University Press.

Leonard, J. (2021). An autobiographical account of desistance and recovery. In Lynch, O., Windle, J., & Ahmed, Y. (Eds.), *Giving voice to diversity in criminological research: Nothing about us without us* (pp. 149–156). Policy.

Leonard, J., & Windle, J. (2020). 'I could have went down a different path': Talking to people who used drugs problematically and service providers about Irish drug policy alternatives. *International Journal of Drug Policy, 84*, 102891.

Loeber, R., & Farrington, D. P. (2012). *From Juvenile delinquency to adult crime: Criminal careers, justice policy, and prevention*. Oxford University Press.

Lynch, O. (2015). Desistance and de-radicalization—The case of terrorism and political violence. In S. Zeiger & A. Aly (Eds.), *Countering violent extremism: Developing an evidence base for policy and practice*. Curtin University Press.

Lynch, O., Windle, J., & Ahmed, Y. (2021). *Giving voice to diversity in criminological research: Nothing about us without us*. Policy.

Makarios, M., Steiner, B., & Travis, L. F. (2010). Examining the predictors of recidivism among men and women released from prison in Ohio. *Criminal Justice and Behavior, 37*(12), 1377–1391.

Marsh, B. (2011). Narrating desistance: Identity change and the 12-step script. *Irish Probation Journal, 8*(1), 49–68.

Martynowicz, A., & Quigley, M. (2010). *'It's like stepping on a landmine …': Reintegration of prisoners in Ireland*. Irish Penal Reform Trust.
Maruna, S. (2001). *Making good: How ex-convicts reform and rebuild their lives*. American Psychological Association Press.
Maruna, S., & Farrall, S. (2004). Desistance from crime: A theoretical reformulation. *Kolner Zeitschrift Fur Soziologie Und Sozialpsychologie, 43*(2), 171–194.
Maruna, S., & Liem, M. (2021). Where is this story going? A critical analysis of the emerging field of narrative criminology. *Annual Review of Criminology, 4*(1), 125–146.
Maruna, S., & Roy, K. (2007). Amputation or reconstruction? Notes on 'knifing off' and desistance from crime. *Journal of Contemporary Criminal Justice, 23*(1), 104–124.
Maruna, S., Lebel, T. P., Mitchell, N., & Naples, M. (2004). Pygmalion in the reintegration process: Desistance from crime through the looking glass. *Psychology, Crime and Law, 10*(3), 271–281.
Massoglia, M., & Uggen, C. (2010). Settling down and aging out: Towards an interactionist theory of desistence and the transition to adulthood. *American Journal of Sociology, 116*(2), 543–582.
Maté, G. (2012). Addiction: Childhood trauma, stress and the biology of addiction. *Journal of Restorative Medicine, 1*(1), 56–63.
McAdams, D. P. (2001). The psychology of life stories. *Review of General Psychology, 5*(2), 100–122.
McAlinden, A. M., Farmer, M., & Maruna, S. (2017). Desistance from sexual offending: Do the mainstream theories apply? *Criminology and Criminal Justice, 17*(3), 266–283.
McCray, K., Wesely, J. K., & Rasche, C. E. (2011). Rehab retrospect: Former prostitutes and the (re)construction of deviance. *Deviant Behavior, 32*(8), 743–768.
McCullough, D., Schmidt, T., & Lockhart, B. (1990). *Car theft in Northern Ireland: Recent studies on a persistent problem*. Extern.
McLean, R. (2019). *Gangs, drugs and (dis) organised crime*. Policy.
McNeill, F. (2006). Community supervision: Context and relationships matter. In B. Goldson & J. Muncie (Eds.), *Youth crime and justice* (pp. 125–139). Sage.
McNeill, F. (2016). Desistance and criminal justice in Scotland. In H. Croall, G. Mooney, & R. Munro (Eds.), *Crime, justice and society in Scotland* (pp. 200–216). Routledge.
McNeill, F., Farrall, S., Lightowler, C., & Maruna, S. (2012). *How and why people stop offending: Discovering desistance*. IRISS.
McVerry, P. (2003). *'Joyriders', The meaning is in the shadows*. Veritas.
McWilliams, D. (2005). *The Pope's children*. Gill.

Merriam, S. B., Johnson-Bailey, J., Lee, M. Y., Kee, Y., Ntseane, G., & Muhamad, M. (2001). Power and positionality: Negotiating insider/outsider status within and across cultures. *International Journal of Lifelong Education, 20*(5), 405–416.

Messerschmidt, J. (1993). *Masculinities and crime*. Rowman and Littlefield.

Mitchell, M. M., Fahmy, C., Pyrooz, D. C., & Decker, S. H. (2017). Criminal crews, codes, and contexts: Differences and similarities across the code of the street, convict code, street gangs, and prison gangs. *Deviant Behaviour, 38*(10), 1197–1222.

Moffit, T. (1993). Adolescence-limited and life course persistent anti-social behaviour; a development taxonomy. *Psychological Review, 100*(4), 674–701.

Mullins, C. W. (2006). *Holding your square: Masculinities, streetlife and violence*. Willan.

Mulcahy, J. (2021). Re-storying offending behaviour: A normal response to an overdose of trauma? In O. Lynch, J. Windle, & Y. Amhed (Eds.), *Giving voice to diversity in criminological research: 'Nothing about us without us'* (pp. 89–102). Policy.

Nugent, B., & Schinkel, M. (2016). The pains of desistance. *Criminology and Criminal Justice, 16*(5), 568–584.

O'Connell, C. (2007). *The state and housing in Ireland: Ideology, policy and practice*. Nova Science.

O'Donnell, I., Teljeur, C., Hughes, N., Baumer, E., & Kelly, A. (2007). When prisoners go home: Punishment, social deprivation and the geography of reintegration. *Irish Criminal Law Journal, 17*(4), 3–9.

O'Mahony, P. (1997). *Mountjoy prisoners: A sociological and criminological profile*. The Stationery Office.

Paternoster, R., & Bushway, S. (2009). Desistance and the 'feared self': Toward an identity theory of criminal desistance. *The Journal of Criminal Law and Criminology, 99*(3), 1103–1156.

Paternoster, R., Bachman, R., Kerrison, E., O'Connell, D., & Smith, L. (2016). Desistance from crime and identity: An empirical test with survival time. *Criminal Justice and Behaviour, 43*(9), 1204–1224.

Phillips, G. (2002). *An empirical study of the intensive probation scheme in Cork: Incorporating a qualitative and longitudinal analysis* [MA thesis, University College Cork].

Pollak, S. (2017, February 2). More than 70% of prisoners have addiction issues, *Irish Times*.

Presser, L. (2009). The narratives of offenders. *Theoretical Criminology, 13*(2), 177–200.

Probation Service. (2012). *Drug and alcohol misuse among adult offenders on probation supervision in Ireland*. Probation Service.

Redko, C., Carlson, R. G., & Rapp, R. C. (2007). A folk model of treatment readiness among drug users in Ohio. *Journal of Ethnicity in Substance Abuse, 6*(2), 15–40.

Robinson, A., & Hamilton, P. (2016). *Moving on from crime and substance use: Transforming identities*. Policy Press.

Roeyen, S. V., Anderson, S., Vanderplasschen, W., Colman, C., & Vander Laenen, F. (2017). Desistance in drug-using offenders: A narrative review. *European Journal of Criminology, 14*(5), 606–625.

Rooney, P. (2005). Researching from the inside—Does it compromise validity? *Level3, 3*(1), 3–19.

Sampson, R., & Laub, J. (1993). Crime and deviance in the life course. *Annual Review of Sociology, 18*(1), 63–84.

Schroeder, R. D., Giordano, P. C., & Cernkovich, S. A. (2007). Drug use and desistance processes. *Criminology, 45*(10), 191–198.

Shapland, J., & Bottoms, A. (2011). Reflections on social values, offending and desistance among young adult recidivists. *Punishment and Society, 13*(3), 256–282.

Seaman, V., & Lynch, O. (2016). Learning the basics of how to live: Ex-prisoners accounts of doing desistance. *Irish Probation Journal, 16*(1), 65–83.

Seaman, V., & Lynch, O. (2022a). Knifing off? Social networks and the inadequacies of desistance frameworks for women in the criminal justice system in Ireland. In S. Grace, M. O'Neill, T. Walker, H. King, L. Baldwin, A. Jobe, O. Lynch, F. Measham, K. O'Brien, & V. Seaman (Eds.), *Criminal women; Gender matters* (pp. 20–35). Policy.

Seaman, V., & Lynch, O. (2022b). Perpetrators and victims: Women, double deviance, and the criminal justice system. In I. Masson & N. Booth (Eds.), *Handbook of women's experiences in criminal justice*. Routledge.

Shapland, J., Farrall, S., & Bottoms, A. (2016). *Global perspectives on desistance*. Routledge.

Shaw, C. (1930). *The Jack-Roller, a delinquent boy's own story*. University of Chicago Press.

Skardhamar, T., & Savolainen, J. (2014). Changes in criminal offending around the time of job entry: A study of employment and desistance. *Criminology, 52*(2), 263–291.

Smyth, A., & Holian, R. (2008). Credibility issues in research from within organisations. In P. Sikes & A. Potts (Eds.), *Researching education from the inside* (pp. 41–56). Routledge.

Sobell, L., Cunningham, J., & Sobell, M. (1996). Recovery from alcohol problems with and without treatment: Prevalence in two population surveys. *American Journal of Public Health, 86*(7), 966–972.

Spector-Mersel, G. (2006). Never-aging stories: Western hegemonic masculinity scripts. *Journal of Gender Studies, 15*(1), 67–82.

Squeglia, L. M., Jacobus, J., & Tapert, S. F. (2009). The influence of substance use on adolescent brain development. *Journal of Clinical EEG and Neuroscience, 40*(1), 31–38.

Stets, J. E., & Burke, P. J. (2000). Identity theory and social identity theory. *Social Psychology Quarterly, 11*(2), 224–237.

Stevens, A. (2011). *Drugs, crime and public health: The political economy of drug policy*. Routledge.

Stevens, E., Jason, L. A., Ram, D., & Light, J. (2015). Investigating social support and network relationships in substance use disorder recovery. *Substance Abuse, 36*(4), 396–399.

Sutherland, E. (1937). *The professional thief*. University of Chicago Press.

Sutherland, E. H. (1949). *Principles of criminology*. Lippinccot.

Sussman, S., & Black, D. S. (2008). Substitute addiction: A concern for researchers and practitioners. *Journal of Drug Education, 38*(2), 167–180.

Tajfel, H. E. (1978). *Differentiation between social groups: Studies in the social psychology of intergroup relations*. Academic Press.

Teplin, L. A., Abram, K. M., McClelland, G. M., Dulcan, M. K., & Mericle, A. A. (2002). Psychiatric disorders in youth in juvenile detention. *Archives of General Psychiatry, 59*(12), 1133–1143.

Tomsen, S. (2008). Masculinities, crime, and criminalisation. In T. Anthony & C. Cunneen (Eds.), *Theoretical criminology companion* (pp. 94–104). Hawkins Press.

Troy, M., & Sroufe, L. (1987). Victimization among preschoolers: Role of attachment relationship history. *Journal of the American Academy of Child and Adolescent Psychiatry, 26*(2), 166–172.

Tyler, I. (2020). *Stigma: The machinery of inequality*. Bloomsbury.

Van der Kolk, B. (2005). Developmental trauma disorder: Towards a rational diagnosis for children with complex trauma histories. *Psychiatric Annals, 35*(5), 401–408.

Van der Kolk, B. (2014). *The body keeps the score*. Penguin.

Weaver, B., & McNeill, F. (2007). *Giving up crime: Directions for policy*. Scottish Centre for Crime and Justice Research.

Welte, J. W., Zhang, L., & Wieczorek, W. F. (2001). The effects of substance use on specific types of criminal offending in young men. *Journal of Research in Crime and Delinquency, 38*(4), 416–438.

White, T. J. (2010). Celtic collapse, or Celtic correction? Ireland's recession in historical perspective. *New Hibernia Review, 14*(4), 27–43.

Willis, P. (1977). *Learning to labour. How working class kids get working class jobs*. Routledge.

Windle, J. (2018). The impact of the Great Recession on the Irish drug market. *Criminology and Criminal Justice, 18*(5), 548–567.

Windle, J. (2019). The causes and consequences of gangland violence in the Republic of Ireland. In R. Lombardo (Ed.), *Organized crime: Causes and consequences* (pp. 110–123). Nova Science.

Windle, J. (2021). Reconsidering the 1991 Blackbird Leys Rioters as an underclass: An insider perspective. In O. Lynch, J. Windle, & Y. Ahmed (Eds.), *Giving voice to diversity in criminological research: Nothing about us without us* (pp. 133–148). Policy.

Windle, J., & Briggs, D. (2015). Going solo: The social organisation of drug dealing within a London street gang. *Journal of Youth Studies, 18*(9), 1170–1185.

Windle, J., Moyle, L., & Coomber, R. (2020). 'Vulnerable' kids going country: Children and young people's involvement in county lines drug dealing. *Youth Justice, 20*(1–2), 64–78.

Windle, J., & Silke, A. (2019). Is drawing from the state 'state of the art'? A review of organised crime research data collection and analysis, 2004–2018. *Trends in Organized Crime, 22*(4), 394–413.

Winlow, S. (2001). *Badfellas crime, tradition and new masculinities*. Berg.

World Health Organisation. (2018). *Alcohol, drugs and addictive behaviours unit*. http://www.who.int/topics/substance_abuse/en/

Index

A

abstinence, 88, 106, 117, 125, 128
addict/ed, 3–5, 14, 31, 60, 118, 119, 137
addiction services, 35, 108
adolescent/adolescence, 6, 126
adulthood, 6, 14, 33, 146
adverse childhood experience (ACE), 46, 59
agency, 14, 16, 139
alcoholic, 50
Alcoholics Anonymous (AA), 17
anti-social, 55, 57, 144
arrested, 91

B

boredom, 7, 52, 53, 64, 77, 138
bullying, vii, 46, 51, 52, 90

C

Celtic Tiger, 6, 25, 26, 75, 77
co-morbidity, 80
confidence, 49, 65, 72, 73, 80, 104, 130
Consent, 41
consumption, 12, 65, 72, 74–76, 79, 83, 85, 88, 93, 101, 102
contagion, 71
coping strategy, 81
criminal careers, 33, 138
criminal justice system, 2, 7, 13, 22, 31, 33–35, 46, 49, 88
criminal records
  conviction, 31, 129
criminology, 6, 11, 33
culture, 12, 16, 19, 38–40, 55, 58, 65, 67, 74, 89, 106, 109, 124, 136–138, 140, 142

D

data storage, 41
deindustrialisation, 6, 24
desist, 13–15, 82, 107, 109, 124, 139, 148
desistance, viii, ix, 1, 3, 6, 12–19, 32, 33, 35, 39, 58, 64, 97, 102, 106,

G. Cambridge et al., *The Desistance Journey*,
https://doi.org/10.1007/978-3-031-11269-0

107, 111–115, 117, 120, 121, 124–126, 128, 129, 136, 139–142, 144–147
deviant, 54, 146
disadvantaged, 14, 24, 27, 38, 39, 46
disengage, 77, 120
disrespected, 69, 71, 120, 122
drug misuse, 11
drug use, viii, 2, 4, 5, 7, 12, 13, 26, 28, 34, 45, 60, 72, 73, 75, 79, 82, 86, 92, 93, 107, 118, 128, 136, 138

E
early childhood, 7, 33, 45, 49
economic deprivation, vii, viii, 2, 6, 26–28, 53, 55, 59, 60, 136–138, 146–148
economic disadvantage, 12, 26, 27, 59
education, 3, 14, 15, 24, 27, 37, 38, 40, 45, 47, 48, 50–52, 54, 58–60, 65, 77, 88, 93, 106, 107, 109, 110, 129, 136
educational attainment, 3, 13, 24, 26, 27, 46
employment
  unemployed, viii, 12, 13, 15, 24, 26, 33, 38, 51, 58, 65, 74, 76, 77, 93, 106, 118, 129, 136, 142, 143
ethics, 41
exclusion, vii, viii, 6, 12, 25, 26, 47, 48, 51, 53, 54, 57, 59, 60, 106, 137, 147, 148

F
father, 49, 54, 70, 84, 92, 99, 125
fear, 49, 68, 69, 78, 83, 90, 104, 107, 112, 120
feuding, 70, 90, 120, 121

G
gamble/gambling, 79
Gardaí, 67, 68, 79, 87
gatekeeper, 33, 34
gateway, ix, 105, 113, 114, 118, 121, 140, 141, 144
gender roles, 65
global
  local, 24, 77
good life, 99, 113–115, 124, 129
grief, 86, 87
Grounded Theory, 19, 31, 32
guilt, 47, 80, 106

H
hard-men/hard man, 7
harm, 4, 5, 37, 47, 52, 64, 68, 79, 81, 84, 86, 93, 123–125
homelessness, 13, 143

I
identity, viii, ix, 3, 6, 14–19, 38, 54–57, 64, 65, 67, 68, 70, 72, 77, 78, 80–83, 85, 90, 93, 94, 98, 101, 102, 104, 110, 113–116, 118, 121–124, 127–129, 136, 139, 141–147
image, ix, 55, 68, 71, 85, 88, 90, 91, 93, 94, 99, 102, 109, 122, 123, 127, 130, 147
imitation, 7, 55, 57
imprisonment, 13, 107
incarcerated
  imprisoned, 19, 27, 60, 87, 92, 115, 141
insider, 2, 7, 32, 38–40, 115
intoxicated, 12, 71–73, 77–79, 86, 88, 138

J
joyriding, 52, 53, 56

K
knifing off, 111, 115, 116, 140–142

L
life history(ies), 2, 7, 31–33, 38, 46
lonely, 99, 115, 118, 121

M
masculinity, vii–ix, 16, 53–55, 57, 58, 64, 65, 67, 68, 72, 78, 80, 83, 90, 93, 99, 102, 109, 113, 118, 120, 121, 123, 124, 127, 136–138, 140, 141, 145–147
maturity, 14, 125, 126
mental ill health/mental health, 64, 80
mocked, 52

N
narrative(s), 8, 15, 19, 28, 33, 59, 63, 103, 136, 137, 145
norms
  values, 15, 17, 55, 56, 72, 138, 146
Northside, 2, 3, 7, 25, 26, 28, 35, 37, 38, 52, 54, 55, 71, 109

O
overdose, 81, 85–87, 105, 139

P
parents, 24, 33, 48, 50–52, 54, 55, 70, 81, 121, 137
performative/performance, 64, 65, 67
persistence
  persister, 33, 146
political violence, 1
poverty, vii, 7, 16, 25, 26, 38, 46–48, 51, 54, 56, 59, 60, 100, 137, 138, 143
power, 33, 39, 53, 57, 65, 66, 93, 104, 130, 147
primary desistance, 6, 144
Probation Service, 37, 74
progression, 77, 81, 82
pro-social bonds, 12, 125

R
recidivism, 12, 88
recovery, viii–x, 2, 3, 5, 6, 8, 13–19, 35, 55, 58, 64, 79, 84, 86, 93, 94, 97, 98, 100–103, 105–109, 111–121, 123–130, 136, 139–147
rehabilitation, 6, 19, 88, 93, 111, 118, 119, 128, 144
reintegration
  integration, 15
relapse, 8, 13, 18, 80, 98, 100, 103–106, 108, 113, 142, 144, 146
reputation, 64–66, 68, 69, 71, 72, 89, 94
resilience/resilient, 8, 19, 112, 146
respect, 4, 65–71, 118, 121, 147
retaliate/retaliation, viii, 68, 69, 71, 123
Revitalising Areas by Planning, Investment and Development (RAPID), 23–26
risk-taking, viii, 12, 53, 54, 101
rock bottom, 14, 18
role model, viii, ix, 7, 8, 13, 32, 50, 53–56, 59, 89, 98, 109, 115, 124, 137, 139, 141

S
script, 16

secondary desistance, 6
self-esteem, 49, 65, 77, 80, 92, 102, 122, 129
self-harm, 64, 78, 85, 144
self-image, 16, 17
self-medicating, 80, 81
Semi-structured interviews, 31, 33
sense of self, ix, 14, 16, 17, 65, 71, 72, 82, 94, 99, 102, 114, 121, 142, 144
sex offenders, 1
shame, 7, 46–48, 51, 52, 71, 100, 106, 107
sobriety, 5, 101, 103, 107, 121, 127, 141
social capital, 60, 88
social control, 15, 54, 142
social identity, 15, 16
social mobility, 25, 65
social network, 115
social welfare, 25, 26, 110
stigma, 7, 46–48, 59, 107, 112
street code
  code of the street, 65, 91
stress, 107, 117, 143
subculture, viii, 12, 55, 117
substance use, 4, 7, 64, 93, 106
suicide, viii, 7, 64, 81, 85–87, 93, 105, 139, 143
supervision, 50, 54, 55, 74, 138
survival, 7, 64, 66, 69, 83, 90, 101, 122, 146, 147

T
tertiary desistance, 6, 107, 144
thrill-seeking, 53, 55
transgenerational, 56, 121
trauma, vii, viii, 7, 12, 46, 49, 59, 60, 64, 77, 80, 81, 84, 91, 93, 99, 126, 128, 136, 138, 143, 146
traumatic life experiences, 3, 38, 46, 49
treatment, 5, 35, 37, 49, 82, 84, 92, 94, 100, 103, 104, 115, 119, 127, 139, 140
12-Step Programme, 8

U
unemployment, 24–26, 56, 75
unskilled
  semi-skilled, 27, 28, 77, 129

V
victimised
  victimhood, 7, 122, 138
violence
  agression, ix, 7, 12, 49, 50, 55, 56, 59, 60, 63–72, 78, 84, 88, 90, 91, 93, 94, 117–119, 121, 123, 124, 127, 136–138, 141, 143, 145, 147, 148
vulnerable, 57, 67, 99, 101, 102, 112, 115, 141, 142

W
weak, viii, ix, 58, 67, 69, 90, 99, 120, 123, 138
working class, 24